SPORT KARATE POINT SPARRING

AN ESSENTIAL GUIDE TO THE POINT FIGHTING METHOD

SPORT KARATE POINT SPARRING

AN ESSENTIAL GUIDE TO
THE POINT FIGHTING METHOD

Ed Yuncza

INDOMITABLE PUBLICATIONS

Trenton, New Jersey

Sport Karate Point Sparring
An essential guide to the point fighting method
By Ed Yuncza

Copies of this book are available in quantity for use at a discount.
For further information, contact:

Indomitable Publications
90 Flock Road
Trenton, NJ 08619
publications@eymartialarts.com
609-558-2274

Editors: Arlene Olla, Nina Malone and Chris Baud
Photographer: Paul S. Kayne
Photo Editor: Christina Yuncza
Book Design/Page Layout: Christina Yuncza
Photo models: Ed Yuncza, Michael Ryfinski, Joseph Crouthamel, Gaby Gonzalez, Erika Rojek, Matthew Friedfeld, Kyle Yuncza, Ryan Yuncza, Christopher Hunt, Joseph Vena, Frank Soltis, Ed Tobie, Arlene Olla, Scott Bentivegna

ISBN 978-0-9838008-0-4

Library of Congress Control Number 2011915623

Printed in the United States of America

Warning - Disclaimer:

This book is dedicated to my wife Christina
and my four children: Kyle, Ryan, Connor and Colin.
They are the center of my life and the source of my motivation.
I love you all very much!

Acknowledgements

I would like to thank all those who contributed to this project both directly and indirectly. You have provided me with the help and inspiration to achieve a lifelong dream–writing and publishing my own book.

For the creation of this project I would like to thank my wife Christina, who was responsible for the book design, layout and photo editing. For editing the text and providing me with valuable feedback, I would like to thank Arlene Olla, Nina Malone and Chris Baud. To Paul S. Kayne, for shooting the photographs used in this book, your patience and attention to detail are most appreciated. I would like to extend a special thanks to the following students and instructors who served as models in this book: Mike Ryfinski, Joe Crouthamel, Gaby Gonzalez, Erika Rojek, Matt Friedfeld, Kyle Yuncza, Ryan Yuncza, Chris Hunt, Joe Vena, Frank Soltis, Ed Tobie, Arlene Olla and Scott Bentivegna.

I would also like to thank all of those in my martial arts family and those who have contributed over my many years of training including: all of my instructors, for their quality training and great experiences–especially Grandmaster Bill Wallace, Master John Graden and the entire "Garage Sparring Group"; all of my martial arts students (and their parents) at E.Y. Martial Arts & Self-Defense Concepts; I would also like to thank my Black Belts and my Black Belt instructors.

Thanks to George Tomko of Innovative Awards Inc., who graciously provided the grand championship trophy used in this book.

Finally, I would like to thank my direct family for their support and understanding on this project. You never let me fall down!

I apologize if I have forgotten anyone.

Thank you all once again for everything.
I hope you enjoy the book!

Ed Yuncza

Table of Contents

진리

Foreward

By Bill "Superfoot" Wallace

23 time undefeated Professional Karate Association (PKA) Middleweight Champion

I started competing in open Sport Karate competition in 1966. At that time, everything was allowed: grabs, throws, takedowns, face contact and even groin kicks. There was no protective padding worn by the fighters. From 1966-1969, there were about 20 tournaments nationwide with anywhere from 150 to 300 adult participants. The largest tournaments of this era included The Long Beach International Karate Championships in California, USKA Grand Nationals in Memphis, Tenn., and the U.S. Championships in Dallas, Texas. By 1970, most tournaments begin implementing the "*no face contact*" rule. If a fighter made face contact, he automatically lost the match. All other techniques were still permitted.

In 1974, I started to compete in full contact kickboxing contests. I kicked well but had to learn how to box to better protect my face. Luckily, I retired unhurt and undefeated. In 1976, I solidified the nickname "*Superfoot*" after knocking out Jem Echollas in the second round with a roundhouse kick to the head. The kick was reported to have been so fast that they had to replay it from multiple camera angles to see exactly what happened. Today, I am retired from competition, but I still travel the world doing seminars and appearances. I love to train, and I will forever. I get paid to work out, and I love it.

One of the greatest benefits I see to sparring is it is just a lot of fun! There also is no better way to work on timing and distance in a fighting context than by sparring. Learning how to hit and get hit back is a big deal because to be successful in competition, you must learn to take it as well as dish it out. The camaraderie I have experienced over the years participating in this activity is another major benefit. I've met most of my dearest friends through competition. The most important thing I have found in all of this, however, is not the winning, but rather the competition itself that has become a lifelong challenge and continuing joy.

I have known Ed Yuncza for a number of years and find him to be a superb martial artist, a great technician and a fine human being. I am proud to call Ed one of my Black Belts and look forward to visiting his school to work out with him and his students as often as I can. His book will provide greater insight into Sport Karate point sparring. He effectively explains the many concepts of how we compete, why we compete and the benefits and enjoyment that come from the competition experience.

Good luck in your training!

About this Book

I wrote this book for two reasons: (1) to serve as a sparring guide for my students and instructors and (2) to add to what I perceive to be a scarcity of published information on an activity that is practiced by so many martial artists around the world. There seems to be much less published material specifically about point sparring compared to other types of sparring and fighting. This text is a means of organizing and documenting my personal sparring strategies, which I have developed over the past 20-plus years. It is my personal approach to point fighting.

Many of the concepts and strategies presented here originate from a variety of sources, including my personal experiences and observations as a student, competitor, coach, instructor and school owner. Over the years, I have carefully integrated concepts, drills and terminology from different systems and applied them to point sparring. You will find my strategies have been influenced by a variety of systems, including Taekwondo and Jeet Kune Do Concepts as well as a variety of Okinawan-, Japanese- and American-based karate systems.

Certain individuals have also directly influenced my sparring philosophy, including Bill "Superfoot" Wallace, Sifu Paul Vunak, Master Sang H. Kim and Master John Graden, to name a few. My hope is that this book will provide something useful for competitors and instructors alike.

The Difference Between Sport Fighting and Self-Defense

Occasionally, people will compare fighting sports to one another and even try to measure the "*street effectiveness*" or the self-defense capabilities of each. Such comparisons are senseless because self-defense and sport fighting are completely different.

All fighting sports are just that: **sport!** Granted, some can be physically rougher than others, but in the end, they all have their own set of rules. There are some broad similarities: all fighters use time limits and fight in specific environments, with specific safety equipment, in the presence of referees against a known, single, unarmed opponent.

However, boxers cannot hit below the belt and can only use punching techniques from a gloved fist. Mixed martial artists fight on padded surfaces and cannot attack the eyes or groin. Kickboxers are not allowed to attack downed opponents. Point fighters stop after each hit and attack with light-to-moderate contact. The athletes consent to fight and the intent is to win, not to kill or maim. Finally, you can always safely "*tap out*" or "*throw in the towel*" the moment you get into trouble. You can't do that in a street fight.

Self-defense is about survival, pure and simple. There are no rules. Self-defense situations occur without notification of attack and when you are least prepared for them. Very often, there are multiple assailants (most of the time out of your weight class) who are more likely to be armed than not. There is also no one there to stop the fight if you get into trouble. The consequences of "*losing*" such an encounter are usually serious bodily injury or death.

Athletes of all fighting sports are to be respected as they all exhibit specific talents, dedication and hard work. A sport is neither better nor worse than another, but simply the personal preference of the athlete. Saying that mixed martial arts are better than point sparring is like saying basketball is better than baseball. Such a statement is subjective, anchored purely in personal opinion.

Keep things in perspective! Sport fighting is recreational in nature whereas self-defense is often a matter of life and death. In each, the mindset, the approach taken, the circumstances surrounding the situation, the way a technique would be used, etc., are as different as night and day. The question should not be, "*How well would this technique work on the street?*" but rather, "*How well can this technique score points for me in competition?*" This distinction cannot be stressed enough.

Preface

The most successful point fighting competitors know how to make good decisions and possess the ability to execute at the precise moment necessary to score. They know what to do against a variety of attacking methods and how to handle different types of fighters. All of this does not occur by accident! It is the result of a firm understanding of strategy and constant practice.

The best competitors never simply throw a random technique and hope it scores and then despair when it doesn't. They understand which techniques are most effective at a specific point of time in the match and they can execute on cue against a variety of opponents.

This book will outline many sound sparring concepts ranging from beginner to advanced levels, as well as drills that will help them work best for you. This book is not about the fundamentals of any given martial arts system or style, but one on strategy consistent with improving your ability to point spar. The assumption is that you already know how to block, kick and punch and have a grasp of stances and footwork consistent with your base system. The techniques demonstrated in this book may look a little different from your system, and that's OK. When watching good competitors participate in open point sparring divisions, it is often challenging to identify their base system (especially in the advanced divisions). This is due to the nature of the point sparring game itself.

The main goal of this book is to convey universal point sparring concepts that work best in open competition. Some of these concepts may work for you; others may not. The concepts that don't, that you choose not to integrate into your approach, can at least serve you by providing insight into strategies you may face in the future.

INTRODUCTION

What is Sport Karate?

Sport Karate, also known as Sport Martial Arts, is the application of competitive martial arts in a sporting environment. It has been around since the 1960s. Sport Karate is generally broken down into two major categories: (1) Fighting Divisions and (2) Forms Divisions. Within these divisions are a number of sub-categories. The Fighting Divisions typically comprise team sparring and continuous sparring. Some of the common sub-categories within the Forms Divisions include weapons forms, musical forms, creative forms and team forms. In addition, some Sport Karate tournaments may also offer self-defense and breaking divisions.

What is Non-Continuous Point Sparring?

Non-continuous point sparring (often referred to as Point Sparring or Point Fighting) is a type of martial arts sparring in which the referee stops the fighting each time an opponent is thought to be hit within a legal point area. The referee and corner judges instantly determine if the hit successfully scored. If it did, a point is awarded to the competitor who landed it. The match then resumes on the referee's command until another hit occurs. Non-continuous point sparring divisions are usually separated by weight, age, gender and rank. Matches are usually 2 to 3 minutes long, and the winner is determined by either total points scored (usually the first 1 to 5) or by total points when time has run out. Ties are resolved by sudden death overtime; the competitor who scores first wins.

Typical matches are single elimination. Once a competitor loses there is usually no further opportunity to fight again. Winners of each division sometimes have the opportunity to compete for an overall sparring grand championship against other division winners. Non-continuous point sparring does not allow the use of full contact attacks. It permits only light-to-moderate contact. The main focus is to score points with quick, well-controlled kicking and hand-striking techniques. Speed, not strength, is the most important factor in this type of sparring. Drawing blood, bruising or knocking an opponent unconscious results in immediate disqualification for the offending competitor. This text will focus specifically on non-continuous point sparring, and will simply refer to it as "*point sparring*" for the remainder of the book.

The Benefits of Point Sparring

Point sparring is enjoyed around the world by martial artists of all ages and is one of the more widely practiced forms of sparring. Its benefits go far beyond the obvious fighting or competitive aspects.

- **Builds Confidence**
  Point sparring helps build and develop confidence. That can transcend the competitive realm and benefit athletes in all areas of their personal lives.

- **Increases Endurance**
  Point sparring is an exceptional cardiovascular workout.

- **Improves Your Reflexes**
  Point sparring helps develop the ability to react instantly.

- **Improves Response Under Pressure**
  The training teaches participants to think, plan and make good choices while under pressure. They become better at considering their options and applying them in stressful situations.

- **Improves Instincts**
  Point sparring helps develop the ability to better sense when to move in and out of an opponent's striking range. This instinct is very valuable in self-defense situations.

- **Releases Stress**
  The combination of the cardiovascular demands and mental focus that is required by point sparring makes it a wonderful stress reliever, as it works mind and body simultaneously.

- **It's Safe**
  Since full-contact techniques are prohibited, serious injuries are rare.

- **It's Fun!**
  Point sparring is a lot of fun! After all, it is a game complete with specific strategy and skill requirements. The more you spar, the better you become, and that will increase the satisfaction you derive from this activity.

Chapter 1:
The Rules

It is imperative to understand that rule variations exist in Sport Karate point sparring. These variations can be fairly minor, such as the required number of points to win or the length of a match, or they can be major, such as allowing leg sweeps or attacks to the head. The core rules–light contact and non-continuous nature (stop/go)–are common to all point fighting events.

It would be impossible to write a single book on point sparring that would cover every potential variation in the rule set. The exact rules of any given match will depend on the organization sponsoring the tournament or the school conducting the sparring exercises. The rules described in this chapter are based on those of the North American Sports Karate Association (NASKA). This book addresses universal point sparring concepts. Some of the concepts presented here may not be permitted at every tournament or martial arts school.

Knowledge of a wide array of point fighting concepts will give a competitor greater insight into point fighting strategy and increase his or her chances of success in this activity. It is absolutely essential that a competitor understands the rules he or she will be competing under before engaging in a match. Rule variations can have an impact on the overall strategy. Do not be blindsided by rule variations; this should also be a part of your training and preparation.

Rule variations in Sport Karate point sparring events are typically found in the following areas:

- Legal point zones
- Illegal point zones
- Legal techniques
- Illegal techniques
- Number of points needed to win
- Length of the match
- Number of points awarded for a given technique
- Mandatory safety equipment requirements
- Size of the ring
- Weight classes
- Division set up (e.g., age ranges)

Sport Karate Point Sparring General Definitions

What is a Point?

A point is a controlled legal martial arts technique scored by a competitor while in-bounds and in an upright position that strikes the opponent with the allowable amount of contact to a legal target area. In some tournaments, all techniques are worth 1 point; in others point values can fluctuate depending on the specific target area hit. For example, kicking techniques to the head are worth 2 points, while kicks to the body and hand strikes to any target area are worth 1 point.

Point Zones

- **Legal Target Areas:** Typically include the ribs, chest, abdomen and head. Sometimes include the face (when wearing proper protective gear) and legs.
- **Illegal Target Areas:** Typically include the spine, back of neck, throat, sides of the neck, groin, knees and back. Sometimes include the face and legs.
- **Non-Target Areas:** Generally hips, shoulders, buttocks, arms, legs, hands and feet.

Techniques

- **Legal Techniques**: Legal techniques are all controlled martial arts techniques that are not specifically listed as illegal. They include all kicks, punches and back fist, knife hand and ridge hand strikes. They may be spinning or aerial in nature as long as they are controlled. Sweeping is sometimes allowed in certain tournaments as long as it is immediately followed up with a controlled striking technique (and depending on the surface type of the ring). Grabbing is also permitted sometimes but generally only for no more than a second or two and must end with a striking attempt. Leg kicks are permitted in some tournaments.
- **Illegal Techniques (Fouls):** These typically include head butting, hair-pulling, biting, scratching, elbowing and kneeing as well as palm-heels, spear-hands, attacks to the eyes, take downs or throws. Also prohibited: ground fighting, stomping or kicking a downed opponent, slapping, grabbing (for more than 2 seconds), uncontrolled blind techniques, pushing and, in some tournaments, purposely attacking the legs.

Length of Match

Generally, matches last for 2 to 3 minutes unless the maximum number of points is scored more quickly (usually 3-5 points).

Contact Definitions

- **No Contact:** This means a legal technique is properly executed but is pulled short of actual contact (usually within a few inches) of a legal target area. No Contact generally is used in some tournaments for head or face targets.
- **Light Contact:** This means there is no penetration or visible movement of the competitor as a result of the contact. In general, light touch is required to all legal target areas to score a point.
- **Moderate Contact:** This means slight penetration or slight target movement. Moderate touch contact may be made to all legal areas except the head (where generally only light contact is allowed).
- **Full Contact:** This is defined as excessive penetration or excessive target movement as a result of the strike. Such contact often results in damage or injury. **Full Contact is illegal in point sparring!**

Warnings, Penalties and Disqualifications

- **Warnings:** Verbally issued by the referee to a competitor who violates the rules during the course of a match. Warnings usually occur before points are deducted or a competitor is disqualified in an attempt to keep the match fair. The first warning issued does not usually result in the loss of points unless the penalty is severe or flagrant. In extreme cases, a violation may result in immediate disqualification.
- **Penalties:** The loss of points due to the violation of the rules by one or both competitors.
- **Disqualification:** When a competitor loses the match due to a violation of the tournament rules. After a certain number of warnings have been issued, a competitor may be disqualified. Flagrant or severe penalties generally result in an instant disqualification.

Causes for Warnings, Penalties and Disqualifications

The following are common causes of penalties:

- Intentionally attacking non-target areas
- Using illegal techniques
- Intentionally running out of the ring to avoid fighting
- Intentionally falling to the ground to avoid fighting
- Continuing to attack after being ordered to stop by the referee
- Excessive stalling
- Blind or reckless attacks
- Uncontrolled techniques
- Displaying unsportsmanlike behavior
- Excessive contact
- Not making an obvious attempt to fight (non-competing penalty)

Chapter 2:
Safety Gear

Proper sparring safety gear is required for participation in nearly all Sport Karate tournaments. Using the proper safety gear will maximize your overall experience, making it more fun and enjoyable. The following is the most common safety gear used in open competition today. Keep in mind that mandatory safety gear requirements will vary from tournament to tournament based on the sponsoring organization and the division you are fighting in (youth divisions generally require more safety gear).

- Cup (for male competitors)
- Mouthpiece
- Foam dipped headgear/helmet (face shields optional)
- Foam dipped gloves (approximately 3-5 ounces)
- Foam dipped boots
- Shin guards
- Forearm guards
- Chest protector

Safety gear includes:
(1.) chest guard
(2.) helmet with protective face shield
(3.) mouth piece
(4.) protective gloves
(5.) forearm guards
(6.) thigh protectors
(7.) shin guards
(8.) standard helmet (without face shield)
(9.) protective foot gear

Chapter 3: Stances

Stances refer to the way a competitor stands when sparring. More specifically, stances involve the body position, foot orientation and weight distribution a competitor uses when in engaged in the offensive and defensive phases of a match. While a number of different types of stances exist in the martial arts, Sport Karate tends to favor more upright stances, with the feet about shoulder width apart. This allows for the greatest blend of mobility and balance. Sport Karate stances also tend to have competitors facing sideways and on their toes, allowing for greater mobility while making them a more difficult, less predictable target to hit. Additional stance variations exist but the following are the most successful for point fighting and ones you might expect to see in most Sport Karate tournaments.

Types of Stances

Orthodox Fighting Stance

In the orthodox fighting stance, your head and neck are facing forward toward your opponent. Your body is on a 45-degree angle. For stability, your feet should be a little wider than shoulder width apart, with the lead foot turned slightly inward and the rear foot positioned so that the heel/toe alignment is facing your opponent. The rear heel is up off the floor and both knees are slightly bent. Your weight should be equally distributed on each foot. Your chin should be down and your eyes up. Your fist should be up, pointed toward your opponent and your elbows should be bent and in tight against your body. Try not to drop the rear arm or let the front hand drift downward. Your lead hand must always be the same as the lead leg. In general, the front hand protects the front side of the body (*"front side"* protection) and the rear hand protects the rear side (furthest from your opponent or *"rear side"* protection).

Side Stance

The side stance is a sideways variation of the orthodox fighting stance. It is a more defensible position for point fighting, as your body is turned sideways, making you a smaller target and better protecting most of your legal target areas. It also has outstanding potential for the implementation of lead leg/side facing type kicks such as round, hook and side kicks. Your feet are at a 90-degree angle parallel to each other and the knees are slightly bent. Your hips and upper body should be turned completely sideways to your opponent with your neck and head turned toward him. The side stance offers greater versatility in the use of alternative hand positioning. Beyond the orthodox guard position, the side stance offers the use of the high guard and the low guard positions as well. Each of these two positions can be used like a shield to protect certain legal target areas.

Hand Positions (with stance)

Orthodox Guard Position

This is the "en garde" position taught to you early in your training. In this position, your lead hand should be at your shoulder level (with the elbow in); your rear hand should be aligned with your sternum. Both hands should be pointed toward your opponent.

Low Guard Position

In this position, the lead arm rests against the lead side ribs and the fist covers the groin area. The lead arm serves as a barrier between you and your opponent. The rear arm rests on the rear side ribs above the solar plexus in a vertical manner with the fist protecting the jaw and the upper body area.

High Guard Position

Here, the lead arm rests against the lead side ribs and the fist is protecting the upper body and facial area. The rear arm is resting along the rear side ribs and the fist is protecting the lower body and groin area. Sometimes you shift your body inward to create additional protection.

Open Stance

This term defines the fighters' foot positioning in relation to each other. Open stance refers to when the fighters face each other with different leads. Specifically, one fighter's right leg is forward and the other has his left leg forward. This means the front of both fighters' bodies (stomach and chest) are "open" to kicks executed with the rear leg.

Closed Stance

This term also defines the fighters' foot positioning in relation to each other. Closed stance refers to an orientation in which both fighters have the same leg forward (left or right leg). Both fighters' bodies (stomach and chest) are "closed" to kicks executed with the rear leg. An attempt with a rear leg from this stance would result in contacting the back area (spine) which is an illegal target area and prohibited in point sparring.

TIPS!

- Ultimately, your stance should be comfortable and work for you, as it makes little sense to do otherwise. Variations in stance as well as hand position are acceptable as long as the fighter adheres to the primary principles of a good Sport Karate fighting stance (balancing between good protection and mobility).
- Use the "shock absorber effect" to help you land properly each time after you kick. This is considered a transitional stance to help you balance and stabilize yourself after you execute a kick. It is especially useful when recovering from head-level or jumping kicks. Because it is not a particularly mobile stance, it should only be held for a fraction of a second until you've regained your balance and transition back to a more upright and mobile stance.
- Always bend your knees to adjust for height variations. Never bend at the back or dip your neck or head to avoid attack.
- Deeper stances offer better balance and stability. The downside is they tend to be less mobile than higher stances. They also tend to telegraph and slow the delivery of kicking and punching techniques.
- Higher stances offer more speed and agility. However, they are less stable and balanced compared to lower stances.

A close-up view of the "shock absorber effect"

CHAPTER 4:
THE TOOLS

The following section describes the most effective hand and foot techniques used for point sparring. It does not describe every potential technique that could be used in the sport. In point sparring, the ability to deliver well-timed, quick techniques is the priority for any fighter wishing to succeed. Speed is the name of the game as the competitor who can successfully land a technique first gets the point. Unlike continuous matches where there is no stoppage between exchanges, point sparring matches stop every time a judge or referee sees a point. Because of the rules in this type of competition, power is less important and, in some cases, too much power can literally cost you a match through a disqualification. All techniques should be executed with speed in mind. Getting there first is everything in this game! As a general rule, front leg kicks tend to be faster and less telegraphed than kicks delivered with the rear leg. Rear leg kicks tend to be more powerful because of the hip rotation, but they are more telegraphed and generally take longer to land.

In point sparring, hitting your opponent first is more important than hitting him hard. Extending your kicking foot when delivering the kick increases your reach (by the length of your foot). This improves your chance of scoring. The extension afforded to you by reaching with the kick allows you to penetrate deeper toward your target. In some cases, not extending your foot at the point of impact could result in missing the target altogether.

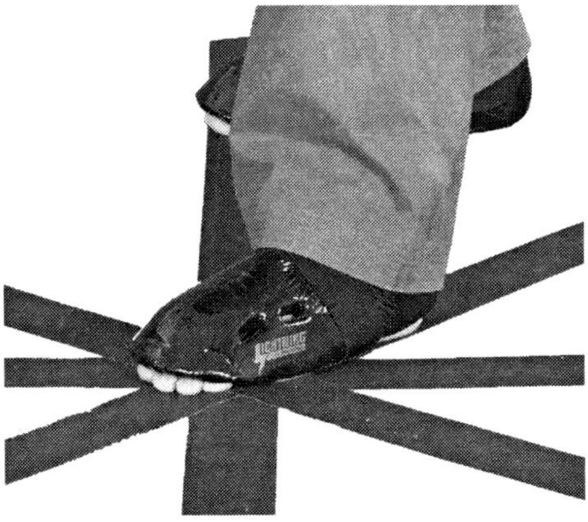

Starting position

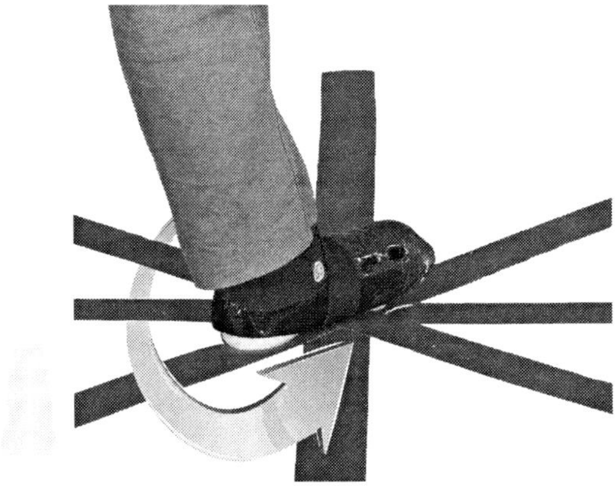

Ending position

To maximize kicking techniques proper foot pivoting is required.
This ensures the best alignment possible for executing the technique.
(A) Pivot on the ball of your foot only!

Foot Techniques

Hook Kick

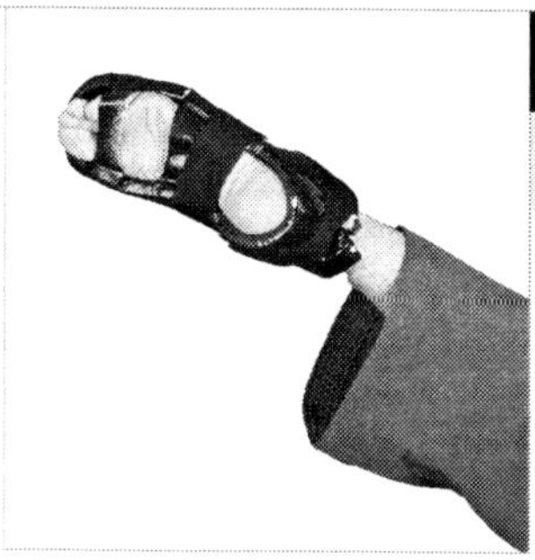

Striking surface

sole of foot

Remember to point your toes for maximum extension/ reach.

Sport Karate variation:

A traditional hook kick (using the heel as the striking point) would miss the target; however, by extending the hook kick (and striking with the sole of the foot), the kick actually reaches the target and scores.

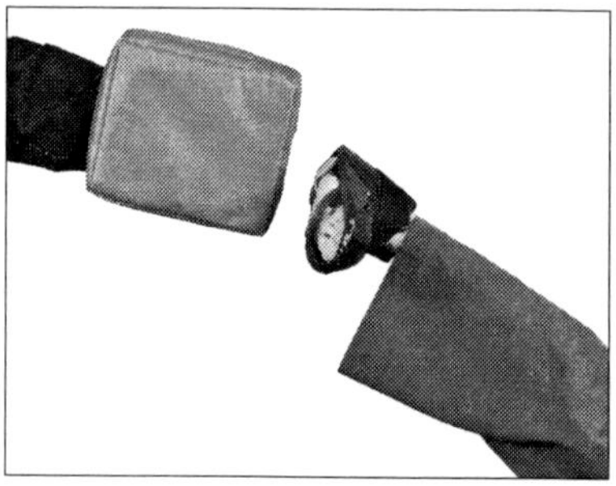

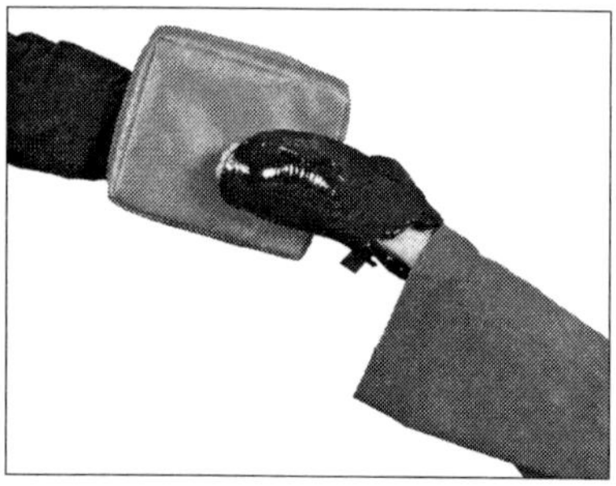

Side Kick

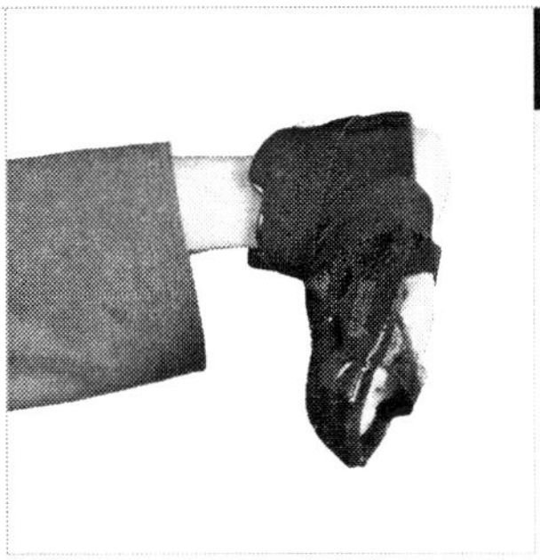

Striking surface
heel

Round Kick

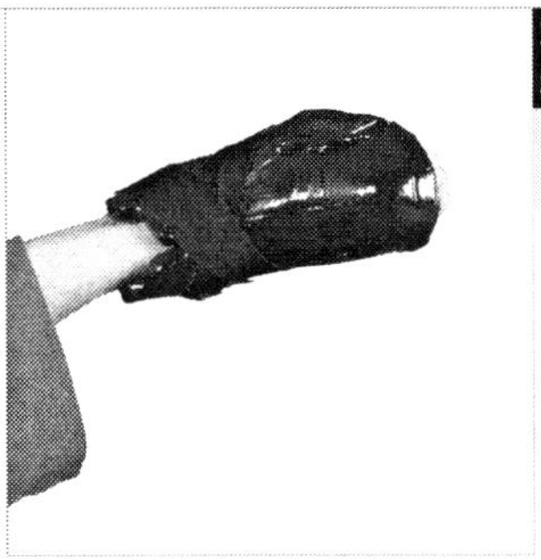

Striking surface
instep

Remember to point your toes for maximum extension/reach.

Front Kick

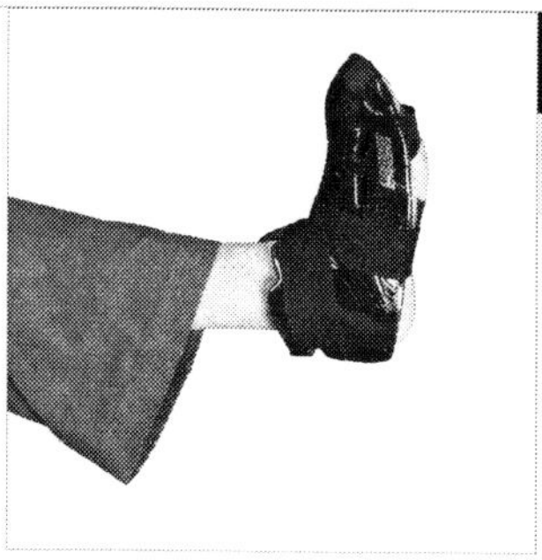

Striking surface

sole of foot

Ax Kick

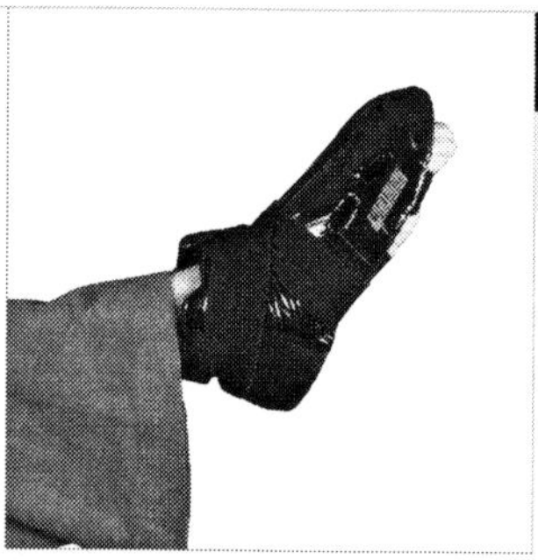

Striking surface

sole of foot

Extend the foot for maximum reach.

This kick is thrown using the front leg in an out- or downward direction. Go only a few inches higher than the target; do not go fully vertical, as it wastes energy and leaves you more open to counter-attack.

Spin Side Kick *(defensive in nature)*

Avoid a blind spinning technique! Remember to always see your target before you actually hit it!

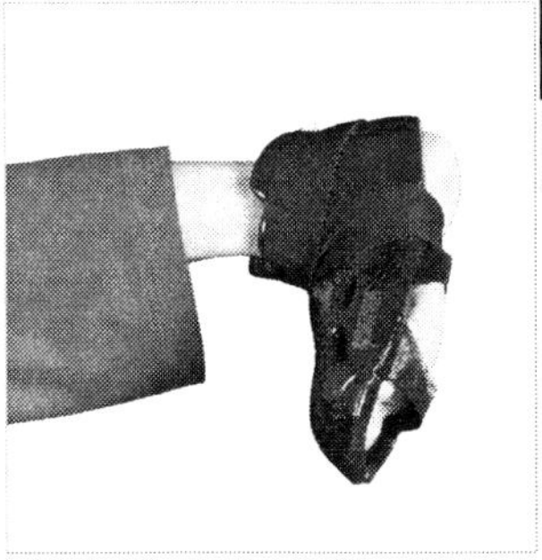

Striking surface

heel or sole of foot

Spin Hook Kick *(defensive in nature)*

Again, avoid a blind spinning technique! Remember to always see your target before you actually hit it!

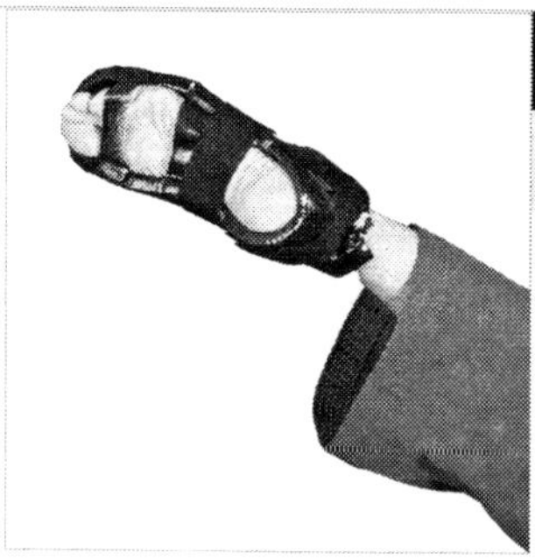

Striking surface

sole of foot

Extend the foot for maximum reach.

Back Kick

Avoid blind spinning technique!
Remember to always see your target before you actually hit it!

Striking surface

Heel

Offensive Spinning Kicks

As a general rule, spin kicks are defensive in nature. They should only be used in counter-attacking situations or at the very least, at the end of a combination attack. The reason is because in order to execute them correctly, you must take your eye off your opponent while you spin. A good competitor will counter-attack when you do this. Offensive spinning techniques work because they begin much farther out of the range of your opponent. They use deception and build such momentum that once going, they are hard to stop.

Offensive Spin Side Kick

Offensive Spin Hook Kick

Double Kicking Variations

Side Kick, High Hook Kick Combo

(1.) *Competitors face off in a closed stance,*

(2.) *fighter throws a side kick to the body,*

Side Kick, High Round Kick Combo

(1.) *Competitors face off in a closed stance,*

(2.) *fighter fires a side kick to the body,*

Hook Kick, Round Kick Combo

(1.) *Competitors face off in a closed stance,*

(2.) *fighter launches a hook kick to knock down his opponent's guard,*

Double Round Kick Combo (low – high)

(1.) *Competitors face off in a closed stance,*

(2.) *fighter executes a round kick to the body,*

Use the same leg to throw multiple kicks (without putting the leg down).
Re-chambering is a critical factor in successfully delivering these kicking combinations.

(3.) re-chambers and

(4.) executes a head-level hook kick.

(3.) re-chambers and

(4.) executes a head-level round kick.

(3.) re-chambers and

(4.) executes a head-level round kick.

(3.) re-chambers and

(4.) executes a head-level round kick.

Probe Kicks

These are any non-committing, low-risk kicks fired from the lead leg to help judge distance, gauge the opponent's reaction and even create openings for scoring. They are sometimes referred to as *"foot jabs."* Kicks that work best for this purpose include front kicks, side kicks and round kicks.

Under Kicking

Under kicking, an unfortunate reality in the kicking game, refers to when to two fighters simultaneously fire a high line kick at each other. The kick that lands first by design will force the kick that lands second to hit somewhere below the target and slide down the kicking leg of the successful competitor. It is not a valid scoring technique and unless flagrant, usually not a penalty either.

(1.) Competitors face off in a closed stance,

(2.) The competitor on the left gets his kick higher than the competitor on the right, resulting in his opponent's foot getting jammed and sliding down into the groin.

Hand Techniques

Back Fist

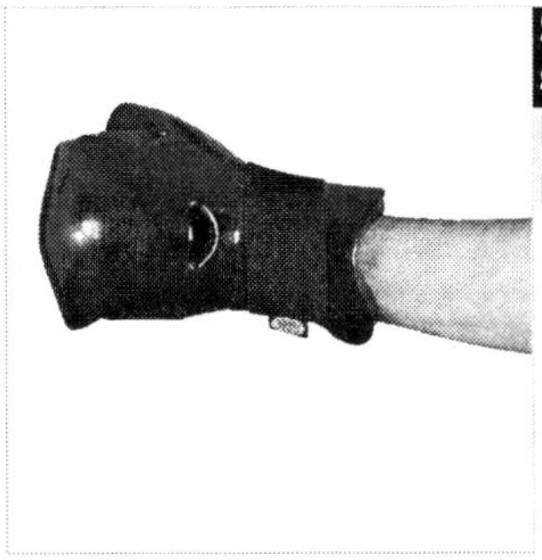

Striking surface
back hand part of the fist

To get full extension, push your shoulders out.

Reverse Punch

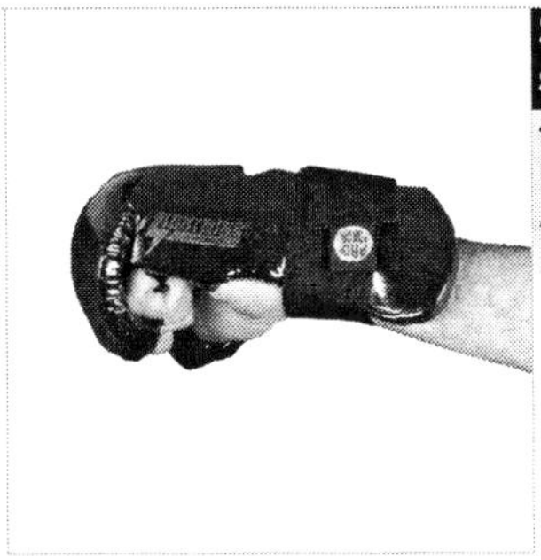

Striking surface
first two knuckles on the fist

Spin Back Fist *(defensive in nature)*

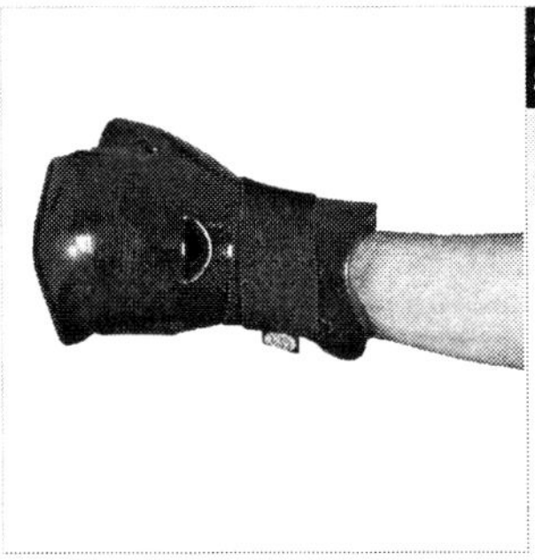

Striking surface
back hand part of the fist

Avoid a blind spinning technique! Remember to always see your target before you actually hit it!

Ridge Hand *(horizontal)*

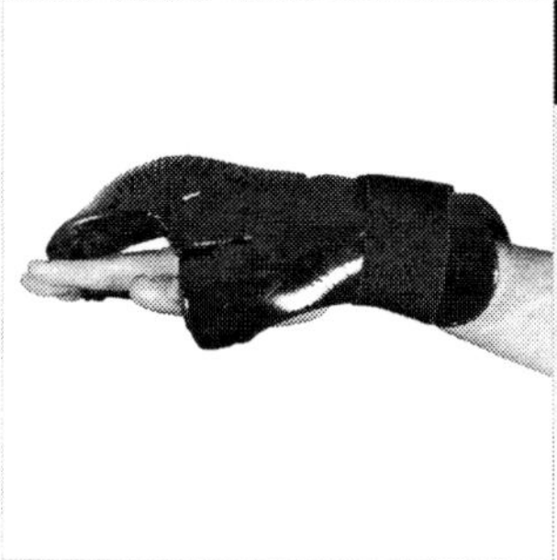

Striking surface

the inside edge of the hand between first joint of index finger and thumb.

Keep your thumb tucked
(so you do not actually strike with it).

Ridge Hand *(vertical)*

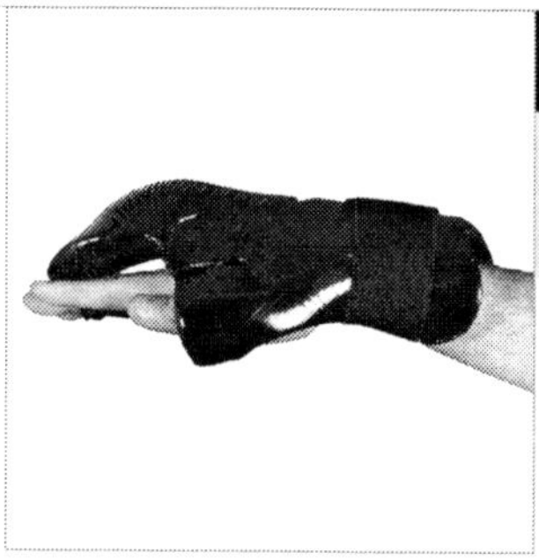

Striking surface

same as the horizontal ridge hand.

This variation allows the technique to be more visible to the officials.

Hammer Fist

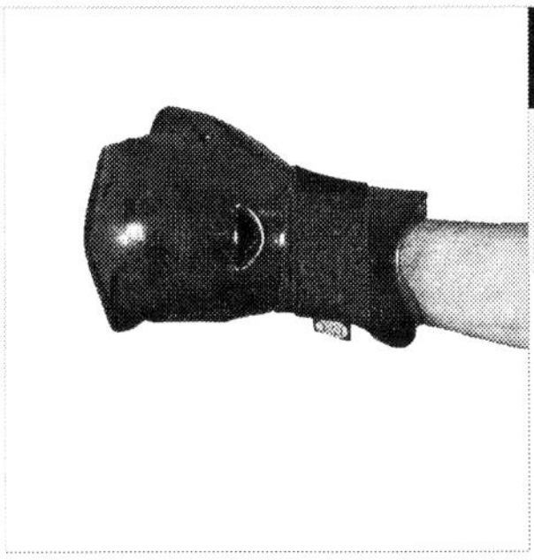

Striking surface

the bottom portion of the clenched fist

Jab

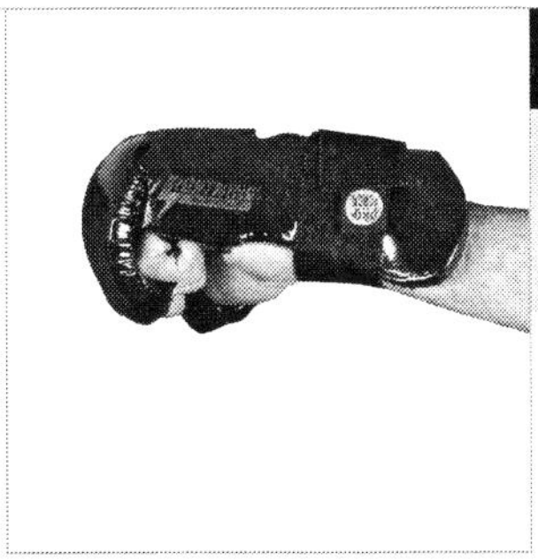

Striking surface

First two knuckles on the punching hand

Chambering

Orthodox Foot Chambering/Re-chambering

The proper foot chamber is the catalyst for any kick. It places your leg in the pre-kick position that ensures maximum effectiveness. It is the equivalent of cocking a single-action revolver: Before you can pull the trigger, you must move the hammer to its ready position. Likewise, before you can kick, you must first cock your leg. Failure to do this results in diminished kicking efficiency. The re-chamber is the opposite of the chamber and is done after the kick has been executed. It is an integral part of successful kicking, but it's often overlooked in practical application. Re-chambering creates an ideal audible snap that results from the combination of the speed of the technique with the proper leg retraction. When done correctly, it enhances the effectiveness of the kick. The chambering/re-chambering described above is applicable to front, round, side, and hook kicks as well as variations on some spin and jump spin kicks.

Orthodox Chambering/Re-chambering Methodology

For demonstration purposes, the side kick is used in this sequence.

Step 1. Chamber the kicking leg, from the floor to the chamber position.

Step 2. Fire the kick at the target.

Step 3. Re-chamber the kicking leg.

Step 4. Place kicking foot back to the ground. Repeat as necessary.

The Modified Kicking Chamber

This approach adds an extra step to the orthodox chambering method. This extra step breaks up the natural kicking rhythm and adds an element of feinting to the kicking technique (which often leads to a higher scoring percentage). This approach can be used at the front end of a kicking attack (during the initial chambering phase of the process) or after a kicking attack is complete (off the re-chambering effort – before you place your foot completely down on the floor). The key is to first lift the kicking leg off the floor, about 12 to 18 inches, as if you were taking a step (this motion will create a reaction in your opponent), then quickly chamber, fire and re-chamber as you would normally do with the conventional style kicks. This kicking modification works especially well in the Sport Karate environment where speed and the first strike is important.

The Modified Kicking Chamber

For demonstration purposes, the side kick will be used once again in this sequence.

Step 1. Lift the kicking leg first (about 12-18 inches off the floor)

Step 2. Then chamber the kicking leg (from 12-18 inches off the floor).

Step 3. Fire the kick at the target.

Step 4. Re-chamber the kicking leg.

Step 5. Place kicking foot back on the ground.

Variation to the Modified Kicking Chamber

Step 1. Chamber the kicking leg, from the floor to the chamber.

Step 2. Fire the kick at the target.

Step 3. Re-chamber the kicking leg.

Step 4. Before you begin to place the kicking leg back down on the floor, quickly re-chamber.

Step 5. Execute a second kick.

Step 6. Re-chamber the kicking leg.

Step 7. Place kicking foot back on the ground. Repeat as necessary.

The Wallace Chambering Method

The Wallace Chambering Method describes a kicking method developed by the most famous kicker in Sport Karate history: Bill "*Superfoot*" Wallace. The Wallace Chambering Method is a subset of the overall "*Wallace Method*" and utilizes the same kicking chamber to fire a variety of different kicks, specifically, the lead leg round house kick, the lead leg side kick and the lead leg hook kick. Each kick has a specific and inherent method for chambering; the problem is each orthodox chambering method by its very design tends to telegraph the kick prior to execution. Being able to associate the chamber with the kick gives the defender a head start on avoiding it. The benefit to using the Wallace Chambering Method is this: The chamber is identical for all three kicks! It is much harder for the opponent to identify which kick is actually being thrown until it is well on its way to the target. The Wallace Chambering Method is all about obscuring the kick for as long as possible, thus giving your opponent less time to react and increasing your chance of scoring.

Side Kick *Round Kick* *Hook Kick*

The Wallace Chambering Method allows for three different kicks to be executed from an identical kicking chamber, making it harder for your opponent to know exactly which kick is coming, until it's too late.

TIPS!

- In competition, use only techniques you have mastered. This may include techniques not mentioned in this book.
- The back fist to the head is generally the fastest hand technique with the highest scoring percentage.
- The most effective fighters use hand techniques to set up their kicks (and vice-versa).
- Maintaining upper body alignment when kicking is imperative. Ideally, your body must be in a straight line with the completed extension of your kicking leg. A common mistake is to bend forward at the waist when delivering a kick. This tends to happen more often when attempting high kicks. This is as disruptive as it is counter-productive; your upper body provides the essential counter-balance for the weight of your kicking leg while it's extended. Bending your body to the side and away from the kick will usually promote the correct upper body alignment necessary to deliver an effective kick while offering the additional benefit of moving your upper body (and head) further away from potential counter-attack.
- The higher you chamber your leg, the higher your kick!
- For better balance while kicking, slightly bend your support leg.
- Re-chamber every time you kick! Don't drop the leg after you are done kicking. Doing so will temporarily take that weapon out of the game (for a second while you recover). It also tends to draw your upper body forward and closer to your opponent, making it easier to counter-attack you.
- Pivot out on your support leg first; this will then allow for the correct hip extension necessary for good kicking. It is also much easier on your knees because if you fail to pivot with your foot, you will invariably pivot on your knee which, in time, will damage the joint.
- Higher kicks generally tend to be slower and more risky than lower kicks. Lower kicks are usually quicker, less dangerous and less susceptible to counter-attack. Using a combination of high- and low-kicking attacks will keep your opponent guessing and maximize your chances of scoring.
- For best stability, plant your base leg before kicking. You should avoid kicking while up on your toes.
- When kicking, make sure your hips are correctly positioned over your support leg. Do not allow your hips to fall out of alignment with the support leg, as this will throw off your natural center of balance and greatly diminish your kicking effectiveness.
- Try to avoid reaching for your opponent with hand striking techniques (particularly with the reverse punch) as this draws you off balance, out of alignment and makes you susceptible to counter-attacks. Instead, use your footwork to bring you closer to your target or, if it's too far, use a kick instead.
- Stay loose and relaxed when executing your techniques. Muscling techniques telegraphs them, makes them slower and uses more energy.
- Round kicks to the body are generally the fastest kicking technique with the highest scoring percentage.

Chapter 5: Blocking/Hit Avoidance

Blocking

Blocking is the action of preventing your opponent's attack from scoring. Generally, this is done by placing the arm or leg across the direct line of attack, which deflects or stops the attack from making contact with its intended target. Sometimes a block can also absorb an attack in a non-point area (such as the shoulders or arms), preventing scoring from occurring. Blocks work best when used in conjunction with footwork and good stances.

Hard Blocking

Uses blocks as intercepting weapons, which hurt the attacking limbs of opponents as they simultaneously prevent the opponent from scoring. Hard blocks meet force with force, but also use rotational mechanics to spread the impact force over a greater surface area to lessen the impact area of the incoming attack (reducing the chance of injuring yourself). These types of blocks are typically "*external*" in nature. Fast and explosive movements characterize external blocking with a focus on physical strength, conditioning and agility. Using hard blocking as a strategy can literally take away an opponent's natural advantage. For example, hard blocks can slow down faster kickers, as most competitors are less likely to continue to kick if they are made to "*pay*" for each kick they throw with a hard block. Also, the cumulative damage hard blocking inflicts can slow down the opponent significantly.

High block

Inside block

Outside block

Low block

Soft Blocking

Uses blocks to redirect and deflect the force of an opponent's attack. Soft blocks do not meet force with force but rather seek to control the opponent's force and use it against him or her. This is done by merging with the opponent's attacking force to control and ultimately redirect the incoming attack. Soft blocks require little muscle strength, but warrant a great amount of dexterity and sensitivity to the movement of your opponent. Soft blocking is typically *"internal"* in nature, which is characterized by the use of relaxed leverage rather than unrefined muscle tension or *"brute force."* Soft blocking is sometimes referred to as *"parrying."*

High block

Inside block

Low block

Press block

Hook block

Outside block

Shield Style Blocking

This blocking strategy involves intentionally absorbing incoming attacks with non-target areas – mainly, the arms or legs – by substituting them for the intended target area. This approach is almost always used with some form of footwork or stance and body shifting and is sometimes used in the recovery process after an attack has been executed. A great benefit to using this form of blocking is it allows for rapid counter-strike capabilities; you are literally *"taking one to give one."* In a Sport Karate context, you are taking one to a non-target area and delivering one to your opponent's target area. The two most common shield blocks used in Sport Karate are the *"universal block"* and the *"shin block."* Others include the shoulder roll, and high, middle and low guards.

Shin Block (vertical and horizontal variations)

The front leg is almost always used for shin blocking, as it is quicker and more direct than the rear leg.

Universal Block

Front View

Side View

Shoulder Roll

Front View

Side View

High Guard

Front View

Side View

Middle Guard

Front View

Side View

Low Guard

Front View

Side View

Leg Raise

Front View

Side View

Shield Combo using Middle Guard and Counter Ridge Hand Strike

(1.) The competitors face off in a closed stance.

(2.) The attacker (left) executes a mid-section round kick, which the defender (right) safely absorbs with a middle guard block.

(3.) The defender then penetrates inward and scores with a ridge hand strike to his opponent's head.

Shield Combo using Universal Block with a Counter Back Fist

(1.) The competitors face off in a closed stance.

(2.) The attacker (left) executes a mid-section round kick, which the defender (right) safely absorbs with a universal block.

(3.) The defender then penetrates inward and scores with a back fist strike to the opponent's head.

Shield Combo using Shin Block and Round Kick

(1.) The competitors face off in a closed stance.

(2.) The attacker (right) chambers for a mid-section round kick, which the defender (left) intercepts with a shin block.

(3.) The defender then executes a high section round kick to his opponent's head and scores.

Jamming

Jamming is a proactive form of blocking that prevents an attack from scoring by using an offensive technique to intercept the attack before it hits a legal target area. It can also work by penetrating through an opponent's range and nullifying his or her ability to punch or kick (basically smothering the ability to effectively attack). The use of shield style blocking along with footwork and good timing make this approach most successful.

Leg Check

Hip Check

Universal Block Jam Sequence

(1.) The competitors face off.

(2.) As the attacker (left) chambers in preparation for his attack, the defender (right) intercepts and jams his effort, nullifying the initial attack.

Press Block Jam and Counter-Attack Sequence

(1.) The competitors face off in an open stance.

(2.) The attacker (left) begins to chamber his lead leg for a kicking attack but the defender (right) steps in and checks the kicking leg (momentarily jamming the technique).

(3.) Before the attacker can regain his balance, the defender follows through and scores with a penetrating reverse punch to the opponent's head.

Press Block Jam and Diving Ridge Hand Attack

(1.) The competitors face off in an open stance.

(2.) The attacker (left) chambers for a mid-section round kick, and the defender (right) steps in and jams with his lead hand (at his opponents shin).

(3.) The defender continues penetrating forward, scoring with a diving vertical ridge hand to his opponent's head.

Leaning

Leaning back as a means of defense essentially gets you out of the direct path of a single volley attack while offering you the opportunity to simultaneously counter-strike. Keeping your guard in place as you do this is critical, because the probability of a follow-up attack is very high and there is always the chance that you can miscalculate the initial attack. Leaning the upper body back while in a low guard position is one of the more common methods used when leaning back in Sport Karate. The rear hand should be up by the jaw to protect the face and head. The front hand should rest against the lead side ribs or hang down and serve as a barrier between you and your opponent. The leaning method is effective because it distorts your opponent's perception of your actual distance. When you lean back he thinks you are out of range. You look like you are farther away because your head and upper body have shifted back, when in reality, your feet have not moved; they are still under your body and very much in attacking range. It is important to fire back quickly after you make the opponent miss. Do not lean back without a counter-technique more than a few times, as this will quickly become predictable and easily countered.

Front View

Side View

It is essential that you keep your hips underneath you when you lean back.
Otherwise you will be unable to immediately follow up with an effective counter-attacking technique.

Leaning can help you avoid initial oncoming attacks (such as reverse punch or back fist). To be most effective, add a simultaneous counter-kick (such as a hook kick or side kick) as you lean back and the initial attack is still occurring.

Ducking

Ducking is a form of hit avoidance in which the athlete evades a blow by suddenly bending, stooping or bobbing underneath it. This method is most effective when used against slower, more committed attacks such as head-level kicks. Against quicker, less committed attacks such as body kicks or nearly any hand technique, other hit avoidance methods are recommended over ducking. Care must be taken not to get hit while in the process of lowering your body. It is essential to keep your hands up and your eyes fixed on your opponent to reduce the chances of getting hit. Quick follow-up attacks (after the initial duck has successfully occurred) are highly recommended and should be considered the second part of any ducking technique.

(1.) The competitors face off in a closed stance.

(2.) The attacker (left) executes a high level rear-leg round kick to the opponent's head, but the defender (right) quickly ducks under the kick while keeping his back straight, his hands up (to protect) and his eyes focused on his opponent.

(3.) The defender immediately springs back to an upright fighting stance and scores with a counter-back fist to his opponent's head.

TIPS!

- Blocking rule of thumb: Never reach for a block or chase a punch or kick. When possible, add footwork to every block and keep your defense in tight.
- Often, Sport Karate players block with open hand style blocks, as this is faster because there is less tension in the arm muscles.
- Never block low line kicks with your arms. This will draw you out of position and make you an easy target for counter-attack. If the kick is lower than your upper thigh, lift the lead leg out of the way or move back to avoid.
- Making the opponent miss is almost always preferable to blocking. Block only if you can't get out of the way first.
- When leaning back, it is essential to keep your hips and support leg aligned to maintain balance and retain your ability to fire a meaningful counter-kick.
- Never block a single attack with both hands. Point fighting is not full contact and using two hands to block creates openings for easy counter-attacking techniques.

CHAPTER 6: FOOTWORK

Footwork is a term describing the general use of the legs and feet in point sparring as it relates to the fighter's movements in and out of the range of attack. Footwork involves balance, distance management and position control. Footwork can also help generate extra momentum for kicks and punches. It is the primary method of hit avoidance in Sport Karate. Footwork is used in distance control (allowing you to move in to jam an attack or move out to avoid getting hit). Good footwork can make your opponent miss you, leaving you in a great position to counter-attack. Making the opponent miss is preferable to blocking because (1) blocking always creates an opening somewhere for the counter-fighter to exploit, (2) blocking can sometimes result in injury to you and (3) making your opponent miss drains large amounts of your opponent's energy and leaves him or her off balance and susceptible to your counter-attack(s). Footwork is a critical element to being a successful point fighter and should not be overlooked or undertrained!

Common Point Sparring Footwork Concepts

Slide Up (back foot moves first)

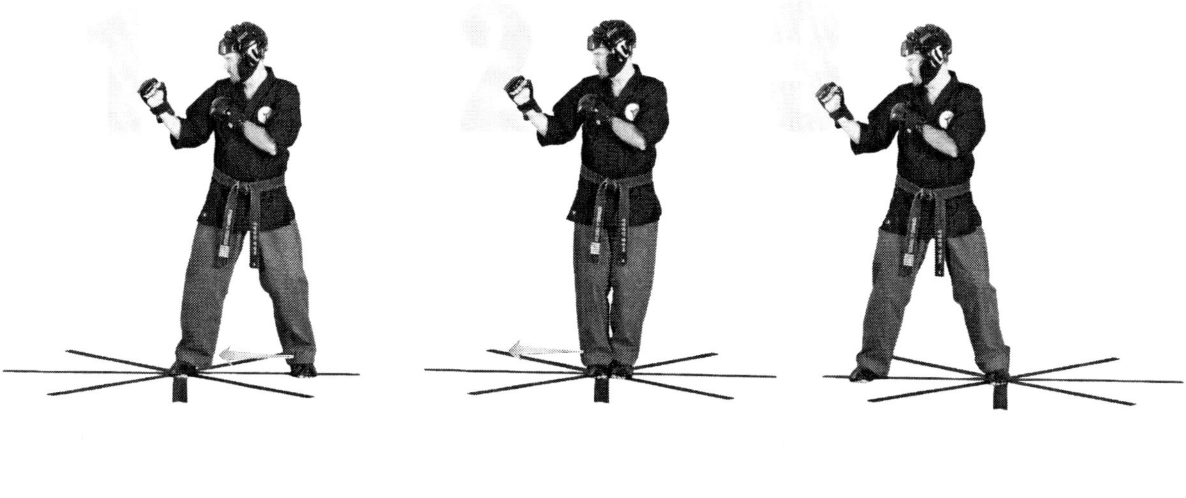

Slide Back (front foot moves first)

Step Up (front foot moves first)

Step Back (rear foot moves first)

Similar variations include: Skip up/skip back and Jump up/jump back (not pictured)

Switch Stance

Half-Beat Switch

Zig-Zag Stepping

Circling "Walking to your Back" **(back leg moves, as you pivot on your front leg)**

Launching into a Blitz-Style Attack

(1.) Competitors face off.

(2.) The attacker (left) sets by transitioning into a modified front stance making sure to position the rear foot correctly.

(3.) Pushing off the rear foot, the attacker launches forward.

(4.) The attacker delivers a back fist to the head. This is usually done when an opponent has executed a technique, missed and is out of position rather than attempting it when an opponent is in a fortified position.

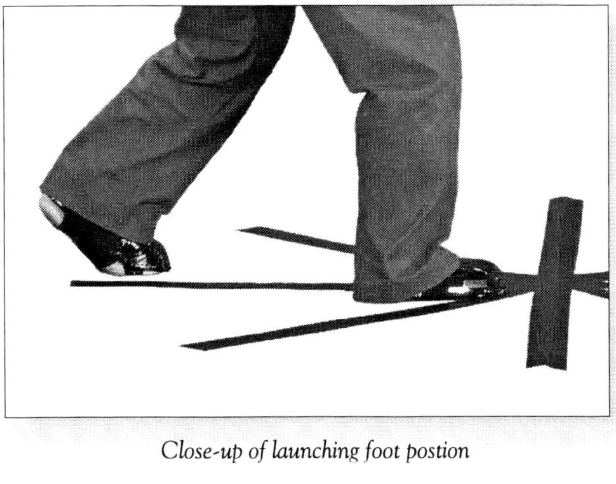

Close-up of launching foot postion

Short Steps/Long Steps

Short steps (as opposed to long steps) give you the chance to safely gauge your opponent's reaction to your movement while at the same time, remaining capable of changing your attack to specifically capitalize on whatever opening has been created by your opponent's reaction to your initial movement (your short steps). Most competitors attack with long footwork. While long footwork is sometimes necessary to effectively move into range of your opponent, it does take longer to complete and while engaged in a long step you are committed (if only for second). Long steps mean more time and, more importantly, they must be completed before a new attack can be initiated. This sometimes takes critical seconds to achieve. Short steps get your opponent to react with big steps; then you know where he or she is going and before he or she can stop or readjust, you launch your second attack, this time knowing precisely where he or she is going to be.

Short Steps

Short steps help to break up rhythm (and help to create broken rhythm)

Long Steps

A Combination of Short and Long Steps

This combination is for better disruption in rhythm

Bouncing Footwork

A rule of thumb generally associated with point sparring is the competitor should try to bounce (be on his toes) as much as possible during the course of a match. This makes the athlete a moving target, which is much harder to hit. In addition, the constant movement disrupts the fight's overall rhythm and makes it less predictable. Attacking from movement also increases the effectiveness of most attacks because the movement makes it harder for your opponent to pinpoint the exact moment the attack begins. In this sense, the bouncing movement helps to hide a technique as it is executed. From a completely static position, any technique is detectible, no matter how fast. However, from movement, a technique borrows from the existing movement and is harder to detect, and hence more effective in scoring.

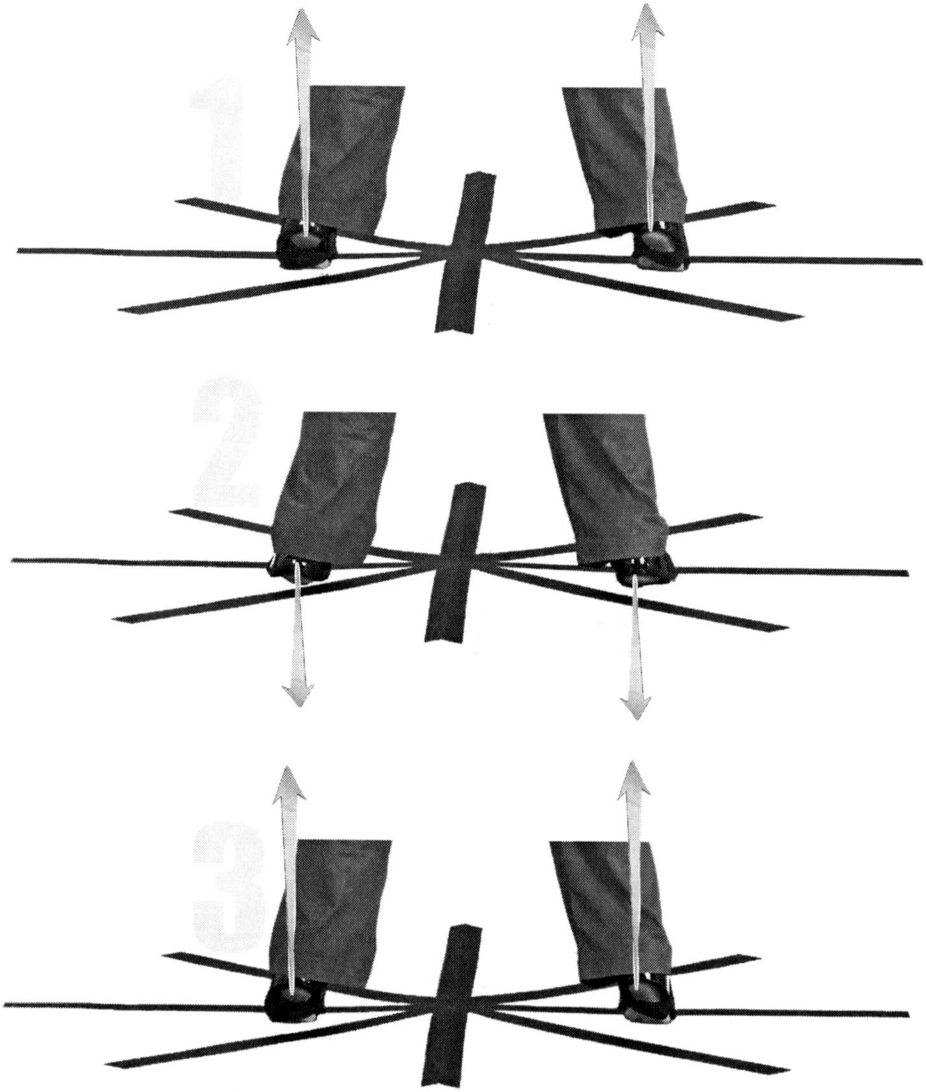

Example of Bouncing Footwork: staying on your toes for optimal mobility also makes it harder to hit a moving target.

Off-Angling

Off-Angling (or zoning) is a footwork concept which, through the use of angles, allows you to move out of reach of your opponent's attack while allowing you to remain in range to launch an immediate counter-attack (in many case before your opponent has had a chance to complete an initial attack). This is sometimes referred to as moving to *"zero pressure"* or out of reach of your opponent's attack. Zero pressure is being where the attack isn't. When that is not entirely possible, it dramatically reduces the effectiveness of the attack. Hit avoidance using off-angling as opposed to moving back on a straight line makes it more difficult for the opponent to hit you with follow-up combinations because you have moved off the initial line of attack. This severely breaks up the attacking rhythm and forces the opponent to immediately recalculate and reposition his stance before resuming the attack. This takes time and allows for excellent counter-attack potential (on your part). Timing is a crucial element in your off-angling strategy because if you move too soon, your opponent will be able to follow you. If you move too late, you'll be scored on. To maximize the concept of off-angling, a fighter should always try to zone to the opponent's *"blind side"* (see page 100) as this will increase the likelihood of a successful counter-attack. A good mixture of zoning out and moving vertically works best in Sport Karate, as it keeps the opponent guessing.

Zoning Against Hand Attack

Zoning Against Kicking Attack

Off-angling footwork must be reflexive; you will not have time to think about it. To be successful, it must be ingrained in both your subconscious and muscle memory. Before it can become a reflex, it must first be understood on a conscious level. Laying out a revised *"Escala Diagram"* on the floor can be tremendously helpful. The Escala Diagram (borrowed from Filipino Kali Martial Arts) models the lines of attack and defense; basically it looks like a big asterisk. It can be painted, taped or even drawn in chalk on the floor. The lines represent the path an attack can travel toward the target as well as the path the target can travel away from the attack. By tracing these lines with your feet, your body becomes familiar with each motion (each angle), increasing muscle memory, relaxation and accuracy. The result will be increased speed and effectiveness in your off-angling footwork. At first, practice on the lines solo. Visualize an opponent attacking as you zone off the attack line. You can even add variations on basic linear footwork that you already know (i.e., sliding, stepping, etc.) as well as adding blocks and counter-techniques. Later, you can work the Escala Diagram with a partner. Eventually, you will not need the diagram. This is when you know you have internalized the movements.

Sometimes footwork alone (without a block) is enough to avoid being hit while still giving you the opportunity to score.

(1). The competitors face off in a closed stance.

(2.) The attacker (right) delivers a side kick, but the defender (left) zones out and avoids being hit.

(3.) As the attacker completes his side kick (and before he can completely recover), the defender connects to the body with his own counter-side kick.

The Escala Diagram

Angles of Movement

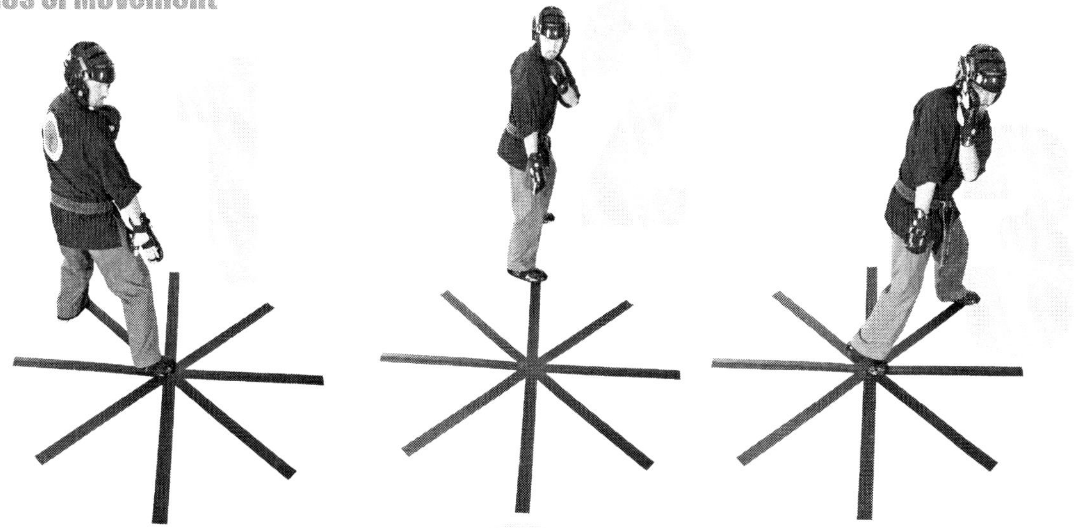

Reference point that illustrates the starting position for all 8 angles of movement shown here.

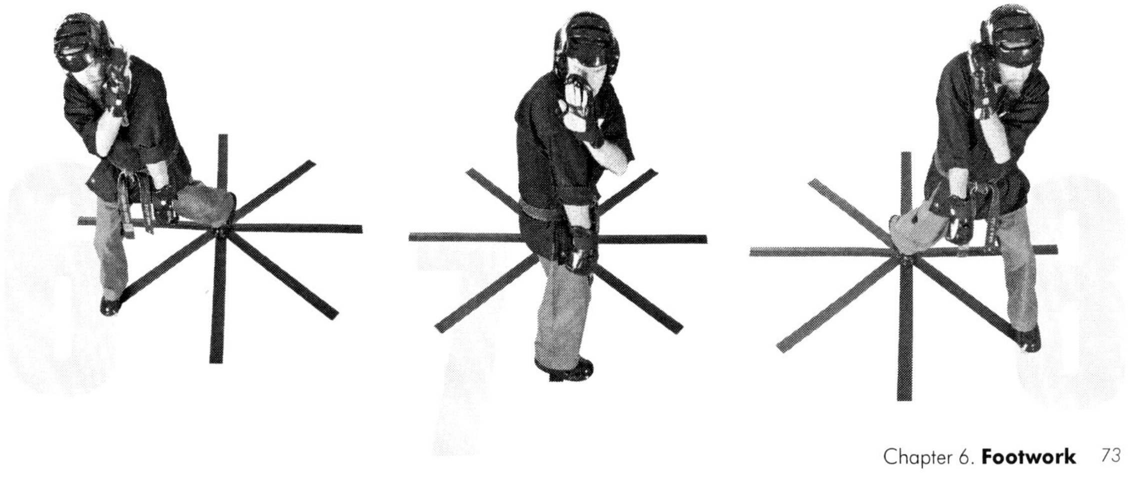

TIPS!

- Evasive footwork is preferable to blocking and should be the first option in defense. If you are not there, you can't be hit. Block only as a last resort, as blocking creates potential openings for counter-attack as well as the potential for injury to the blocking limbs.
- Footwork is the personal preference of any fighter. Use footwork that is comfortable for you and that complements your fighting style and overall approach.
- You should always be up on your toes and moving while point fighting. A moving target is harder to hit and harder to read because it forces your opponent to constantly recalculate the attack.
- Bouncing movement should stop only long enough for you to set and fire your attack. Once that has been done, you should immediately begin to move again.
- Avoid prolonged periods of standing still in a match. Even in a guarded position, the lack of motion will make you a sitting duck for a combination type attack.
- Remember that lack of movement (standing still) helps telegraph any attack you may launch regardless of how fast it is thrown. From a dead stop, any motion, no matter how quick, is much easier to detect. If it can be easily detected, it can be avoided or countered by your opponent.
- Footwork should always be light, smooth and fluid. Avoid choppiness or heavy, dragging types of footwork.
- When adding footwork to your attacks, try to keep your head consistently level during the entire course of the attack. Do not bob up and down, as that telegraphs your intentions and disrupts both flow and balance.
- Try to avoid unnecessary movement that telegraphs your attacks. Things like hopping straight up before attacking, adding extra steps before kicking, excessive foot shuffling, dropping your hands as you move in, etc., all telegraph your intentions and add precious time to your attack (or defense)–time that you cannot afford!
- Smooth (and balanced) footwork is more important than fast footwork.
- Always keep your hands moving when applying any kind of footwork. It gives your opponent more to have to think about.
- Good footwork requires the entire body to move as a single unit; avoid segmented movement.
- When incorporating entering footwork with kicking and punching techniques you should lead with the rear foot first (for sliding or skipping style attacks). This is a real game changer because you get your opponent to react to your movement (so you know what he is going to do and specifically where he is going to be) before you actually launch the kick or the punch.

Chapter 7:
Putting it All Together:
Using the Tools with Blocking and Footwork

Kicking Variations Created by Footwork

Applying good footwork to your kicks can improve their overall effectiveness both offensively and defensively in sparring. Good footwork adds more power, better penetration, greater height and reach and can sometimes serve as a feint. Adding footwork and kicks together also creates variations to basic kicks, which essentially adds additional techniques to your arsenal. A basic, static lead leg side kick can suddenly become a sliding, stepping, bouncing or skipping kick with just a little added footwork. This can effectively turn a single kick into eight kicks if you factor in all possible offensive and defensive variations. The following footwork/kick variations can be used with nearly any lead leg kick. Again, try to avoid telegraphing motions such as head bobbing, excessive foot shuffling, staring at your target or dropping your hands before you deliver the technique.

Bounce Kicking

This variation is similar to what the feet do during jumping jack exercises. Here, both feet come together and at that point, the kick is launched. The best kicks to use with this technique are side facing-style kicks such as the side kick, round kick and hook kick. Bounce kicking distorts your opponent's distance perception. It also requires space to effectively execute. This is one of the few variations that is exclusively offensive in nature.

1

2

3

Step/Skip Kicking: Offensive version

The front foot steps toward the target and is simultaneously chambered. The rear foot drags behind, gliding on the ground, never losing contact with the floor. In this kicking variation, you are literally stepping into your attack. Since you are stepping toward your opponent, this variation requires more space.

Step/Skip Kicking: Defensive version

The rear foot steps away from the target while simultaneously chambering and executing the kick with the front foot. In this kicking variation, you are literally stepping away from your opponent.

Skip/Jump Kicking:
Offensive version

Mechanically very similar to the step kicking variation except the rear foot follows the front foot by skipping forward and slightly leaving the ground (as opposed to dragging behind). This is a good way to safely close the gap and cover distance. Care should be taken to avoid crossing the legs during the skip kick. Although crossing the legs is the more traditional method for delivering this kick, it is less desirable for Sport Karate because it leaves you momentarily less balanced (as your legs are crossed) than the method described here.

Skip/Jump Kicking: Defensive version

First, the rear foot skips backward and away from the incoming opponent while the lead foot is chambered and executes the kick. This is a good way to create kicking distance as an opponent enters.

1

2

3

Slide Kicking:
Offensive version

In this variation, the rear non-kicking foot moves first, sliding to the front foot. Once the two feet make contact, the front foot begins moving forward into a chamber and then quickly to the kick. Moving the rear foot first makes a dramatic difference in how your opponent perceives your attack because it distorts distance perception. In this kicking variation, you have essentially taken a step forward and are closer to the target without your opponent fully realizing it.

Slide Kicking: Defensive version

The front foot first moves back toward the rear foot. Once the two feet make contact, the front foot chambers and kicks in place toward the incoming target. The mechanics of this variation are the opposite of its offensive counterpart. However the result is the same: your opponent's distance perception is distorted by your foot movement. In this case, you have obliquely increased your distance from your opponent, and that gives you much-needed kicking space as the opponent moves toward you.

Footwork Improves your Blocks

Good footwork also improves your blocks by distributing the *"responsibility"* between your block and your footwork. Footwork together with blocking moves you out of an attacker's effective range, rendering it slower and less powerful and thus easier to block or avoid. This concept works both offensively and defensively. The defensive approach usually involves moving away from an attack, drawing out much of its speed and power. Moving back automatically decreases the power of the attack because you are moving away from the point of impact. This makes it much easier to block, avoid and ultimately counter. If the opponent has thrown a committed attack and you move away from the point of impact, the opponent may have to *"reach"* in order to hit you. This *"reaching effect"* greatly reduces the effectiveness of any technique thrown because it throws off the natural balance of the attack. If the opponent is less than completely committed, he or she will most likely attempt to redirect the attack once he or she sees you have moved back. This, too, reduces the effectiveness of the attack by drawing out both power and speed. The block used in that situation becomes redundant just in case your footwork was less than 100% effective in avoiding the hit. The flipside to this concept, the offensive approach, is to step into an attack with your block. In that case, the combination of your footwork and blocking becomes a jam that short-circuits the attack by removing the space required to effectively execute the attack.

Footwork Improves your Blocks

Blocking a kick with no movement/footwork – results in being hit.

Blocking a kick with movement/footwork – despite the kick penetrating more than expected, no point is scored because the athlete used footwork with his blocking.

Footwork Improves your Blocks

Blocking a punch without movement/footwork – results in being hit.

Blocking a punch with movement/footwork – despite the punch reaching full extension, no point is scored because the athlete used footwork with his blocking.

Hand Movement in Conjunction with Bouncing Footwork

Moving your hands around while you spar distracts your opponent. It also forces him to monitor another set of potential weapons. The more that needs to be monitored, the less effective the monitoring is overall (which improves your chance of scoring). Try not to move your hands in a discernable pattern or rhythm; instead, maintain a broken rhythm and occasionally execute legitimate hand attacks. By doing this, your hands will remain a credible threat throughout the duration of the match. Also, make sure you keep your hands in a defensible position while you move them – do not flail them too far out of position as that allows a potential scoring opportunity for your opponent. The main objective with this approach is to overload your opponent's senses and his ability to effectively monitor your full attacking potential.

Side-to-side hand movement.

Up-and-down hand movement.

Chapter 8: Other Necessary Sparring Elements

THE FOLLOWING APPLY BOTH TO OFFENSE AND DEFENSE!

Timing

This is one of the most important factors in sparring. Knowing when to attack and when to defend is a decision-making process. Timing is a critical intangible that is linked to every other aspect of sparring. The more you spar, the better your sense of timing will become. Timing can be a great equalizer as it can enable a slower fighter to score on a faster opponent by knowing when best to attack or defend. Timing is a critical factor in counter-sparring; without it, counter-fighting is impossible to execute.

Rhythm

Refers to measured movements through a space. It is a discernible pattern, which is capable of being monitored. All competitors possess a natural rhythm that they follow when sparring. Some have a very slow rhythm, others have a quicker pace. Some competitors have a predictable and balanced rhythm, while others have one that is harder to understand or follow. Often, opponents can unintentionally affect each other's rhythm. Skilled competitors can dictate the rhythm of a match. Gaining control of the rhythm of the match means that you force the opponent to react to your movements, which puts you in control of the match. A strategy often used by successful fighters is to purposely slow down the action. On the other hand, if you are in better physical condition, then you can force a faster pace to wear your opponent down. Once you do that, you begin to cancel out your opponent's strengths due to fatigue. Ideally, the rhythm of a match should vary, from fast to faster to slow back to fast; by doing that you control the fight by throwing off your opponent's reaction time.

Broken Rhythm

This involves intentionally interrupting your natural rhythm with the intent to distort your opponent's sense of timing, bringing him or her out of phase with you. Broken rhythm by design seeks to be random and difficult to discern.

Distance

Refers to the amount of space between you and your opponent or where you are in relation to your opponent. Distance is a variable and will change constantly during the course of a match. Distance will also dictate the types of techniques that can be used (or not used) based on the four ranges of sparring (see Chapter 9). The skilled fighter understands and monitors distance in every phase of the match and knows how to properly move in and out of the opponent's range without getting hit.

Critical Distance Point

A term coined by Bruce Lee. The critical distance point refers to the farthest position your opponent can be from you and still effectively score (or hit you). It is measured using the longest effective weapon brought to the engagement. For the purposes of Sport Karate it would typically be the opponent's rear leg round kick. The critical distance point is in a constant state of flux during the match. Because of footwork and other movements associated with sparring, it will also be different for every opponent you face (due to variations in their physical size). The goal of a successful competitor is to be constantly aware of the critical distance point and to remain just outside of it during the majority of the match, except when attempting to score. Keen understanding and awareness of the critical distance point also offers excellent defensive scoring opportunities, as you can sometimes literally have your opponents running into your foot or fist because they misjudged their position in relation to yours.

An example of critical distance point against a kicking technique.

An example of critical distance point against a punching technique.

Methods of Effectively Closing the Distance

- Use probe kicks to help determine and then close the distance on your opponent. The reaction to your probe will also give you a better idea about the type of fighter you are facing (See chapter 12 for a description of a Runner, a Blitzer or a Counter-fighter).
- Blitzing is a common method used in point fighting to close the distance between two fighters. The back fist almost always leads any blitz. Blitzing starts out of a bouncing motion (non-static) and should be done when the opponent is out of position (as a result of your footwork). Attempting to blitz an opponent who is ready or waiting for it often fails.
- When your footwork brings you too far outside the critical distance point, use jumping kicks to bring you back into range and score. For example, the distance created by switching your stance to avoid an over-penetrating rear leg kick can be made up by an immediate jumping side kick follow-up.

Examples of Safely Closing the Distance (Bridging the Gap)

(1.) The competitors face off in an open stance.

(2.) The attacker (left) delivers a mid-section rear leg round but the defender (right) avoids this kick by switching stance away from the attack.

(3.) The defender's initial movement (to avoid being hit) has left him too far out of range for a simple counter-kick.

(4.) The defender opts to utilize a quick jumping side kick to his opponent's head to properly bridge the gap.

Examples of Safely Closing the Distance (Bridging the Gap)

(1.) The competitors face off in an open stance.

(2.) The attacker (right) feints a kicking attack by quickly chambering his lead foot.

(3.) The defender (left) reacts to the feint by moving back, thus creating space.

(4.) Before the defender can complete his retreat, the attacker follows up with a rear leg round kick to the body.

Feinting

Feints are deceptive movements designed to mislead or distract your opponent by conveying the impression that a certain attack is being delivered to specific target; feints are merely a distraction from the real points of attack. The main objective of feinting is to create scoring opportunities by opening your opponent's defenses. Good feinting creates a reaction to a phantom attack(s), which then leaves other point zones unprotected and available for scoring.

(1.) The competitors face off in an open stance.

(2.) The attacker (right) feints an attack through a chambering motion.

(3.) The defender (left) reacts to the feint.

(4.) The attacker quickly takes advantage of the opportunity created by his feint and delivers a round kick to his opponent's head.

Hand Feint

From a fighting stance quickly move forward, throw your lead hand out to further confuse your opponent and then move with equal intensity back to the point where you began. The back foot does not move at all during this sequence.

Body Feint

From a fighting stance, quickly shift into a front stance while protecting your upper body with the simultaneous execution of an "*L*" Block, and then quickly shift back to your starting position.

Kick Feint

From a fighting stance, chamber your lead leg for a kick while simultaneously sliding forward on your rear leg. This gives the opponent the impression that a kicking attack is imminent and creates a scoring opportunity on the high line, which you can quickly take advantage of by executing a back fist or a high block (trap) reverse punch combination.

A common follow-up to the kick feint: the backfist-reverse punch combination.

Feinting Factors to Consider

- Feint only if you intend to attack.
- Be careful not to feint in a way that leaves you overly vulnerable for a counter-attack.
- It is important not to become predictable with your feints as it diminishes their effectiveness and leaves you open to counter-attack.
- Feints need to be convincing, otherwise your opponent will ignore them. A feint should be completely indistinguishable from a genuine attack.
- Do not feint when you are clearly out of range or employ a half-effort.
- Consider using audio-style feints. Loud kiaps or hissing sounds can often draw your opponent out of position the same way a physical movement could. For the best result, try mixing both physical feinting motions with audio-style feinting.

Economy of Motion

Is a concept borrowed from Bruce Lee's Jeet Kune Do Concepts martial arts system that seeks to waste as little time or movement as possible when attacking or defending. It teaches that the simplest things work best in both offense and defense. The Economy of Motion concept helps an athlete conserve both energy and time, two crucial components in competition. Economy of Motion strives to be efficient, by using attacks that reach their target(s) in the least amount of time and with the least amount of effort; simple, using uncomplicated thinking without ornamentation, and direct, by proceeding to the target in a straight line or by the shortest course possible.

Economy of Motion Example

(1.) The competitors face off in an open stance.

(2.) The attacker (left) enters with a jab and the defender (right) deflects the punch with an outside pressing block.

(3.) Immediately using the same hand that blocked, the defender follows up with a back fist attack.

(4.) This is followed by a reverse punch to the head.

The "Overload Principal": Simultaneous Blocking-Striking and Footwork

The Overload Principal is nothing more than effectively applying multitasking to sparring. Multitasking, or the ability to work at several different tasks simultaneously, is a valuable skill. The ability to successfully multitask in a fight dramatically improves your chances of winning. This strategy is used by many successful fighters to "*overload*" the opponent with so many things at once that the opponent simply cannot account for everything at one time and gets hit. In point sparring, this is often accomplished by using simultaneous blocking-striking and footwork. When the opponent attacks, you zone out, block and strike all in one motion. The Overload Principal is most effective when applied as your opponent is in the act of attacking; mentally, your opponent thinks he is in control of the fight and is less likely to be thinking defense. In essence, you instantly turn "*the hunter*" into "*the hunted*".

(1.) Competitors face off in an open stance.

(2.) The attacker (left) executes a mid-section rear leg round kick. The defender (right) simultaneously off-angles, blocks (with a lead hand outside pressing block) and executes a reverse punch to his opponent's body.

(1.) The competitors face off in a closed stance.

(2.) The attacker (right) executes a high-section kicking attack with his rear leg. The defender (left) simultaneously steps in, blocks (an outside knife hand block) and executes a horizontal ridge hand strike to his opponent's body.

(1.) The competitors face off in a closed stance.

(2.) The attacker (left) attacks with a lead hand jab. The defender (right) responds by launching a simultaneous step-in block and punch attack, which overloads his opponent's defenses, and scores. This is considered a "classic" Sport Karate technique because of its effectiveness.

Blind Spot Concept

The *"Blind Spot"* refers to a strategic position of advantage in sparring in which the opponent has the least amount of visibility to an oncoming attack. The blind spot position is located to the outside left or right of the defender's ear, depending on whether the athlete's stance is open or closed. Attacking toward the defender's blind spot affords him much less time to react to your attack because the delivery is obscured for the majority of the attacking process, which significantly increases your probability of scoring. In essence, it gives your opponent too little time to effectively react to your attack. Attacking the blind spot is the preferred method of good tournament fighters. Incorporating this strategy into your daily training is highly recommended.

(1.) Attacking to the blind spot essentially conceals your movements long enough into the process of attacking that by the time the defender realizes an attack has been launched, it is too late to stop.

(2.) In contrast, when attacking from the more direct frontal path, the attack is detected much earlier in the process, which generally results in a failed scoring effort.

Chapter 9: The Four Ranges of Sparring

Bruce Lee, the most influential martial artist of the 20th century, categorized four basic ranges used in unarmed combat. It is important to be familiar with these ranges and even more important to understand how to correctly and effectively transition from one range to the next without being scored upon in the process. Secondly, recognizing when you are out of range for a specific attack and adjusting properly is a crucial element in successful point sparring.

The four ranges are:

- **Kicking Range** – This is the farthest range of the four and refers to the distance necessary to deliver strikes using the leg or the foot.
- **Punching Range** – Refers to the distance necessary to deliver strikes using the arm or the hand.
- **Trapping Range** – This range is too close for your opponent to effectively kick or punch. In this range hand and foot immobilization is used along with knees, elbows and foot stomps (all of which are illegal techniques in Sport Karate). Trapping is usually accomplished by temporarily pinning or grabbing an opponent's limbs and simultaneously following up with short range strikes while the opponent is immobilized (and unable to escape) by the initial trapping motion. Trapping Range is sometimes referred to as *"clinch range"* (as in boxing).
- **Grappling Range** – This is the closest range of the four and can include throws, clinching, takedowns and submission holds such as chokes and joint locking (all of which are not permitted in most Sport Karate tournaments). Sometimes referred to as *"wrestling range,"* it can occur when competitors are standing or on the ground. Most Sport Karate tournaments do not allow grappling techniques and will break, then reset the action if the competitors enter this range.

Although Bruce Lee defined four ranges of combat, most point fighting matches focus mainly on the "*Kicking*" and "*Punching*" ranges. Exceptional competitors possess the ability to apply kicking and punching techniques when out of their natural range (especially when they are too close). For example, being able to kick while in punching range very often catches an opponent off guard and offers a quick scoring opportunity. This requires exceptional kicking technique, speed and flexibility. The importance of knowing and understanding these ranges cannot be overstated. To be a successful point fighter, you must train to properly transition between these ranges effectively and deliver your attacks from the proper distance. Too many fighters get scored on because they misjudge their distance and attack from the incorrect range.

Properly Bridging the Gap

It is essential for the point fighter to know how to properly move in and out of the four ranges of sparring. *"Bridging the gap"* is an effective method for safely moving from kicking range to punching range.

(1.) The competitors face off in a closed stance.

(2.) The attacker (right) bridges the gap with a skip front kick to which the defender (left) responds with an ill-advised use of both hands to block a single technique.

(3.) The defender, having committed both hands to his initial defense, has left his high line completely unprotected, which the attacker takes full advantage of by delivering a reverse punch to his opponent's head.

Chapter 10: Offense

Offense is the act of attacking or engaging an opponent with the objective of scoring points. Offense can be direct or indirect (as in the form of counter-fighting).

Key Factors in Offense

- Always keep your hands moving. It is an additional element your opponent has to monitor. Because it splits your opponent's attention, it improves kicking effectiveness and makes scoring easier for you.
- Do not underestimate the value of a punch (especially a stepping punch). The punch is a great *"attention getter"* and if it does not directly score it almost always creates an opening for a second attack. It is also generally faster and more economical than a kick.
- An offensive technique can begin with a defensive move; in fact, you are in a constant flux between offense and defense (it is a volley).
- Always have a reliable (safe) follow-up technique, especially to your kicks. It should be a simple and direct technique such as a jab or back fist.
- Don't stop until the referee calls for a break. Even if you think you scored, the match is still on until the referee calls for a stop.
- Always adhere to the *"follow-up principal."* It is important to be able to follow up with at least 3-5 flurry style techniques. If you can't score in 3-5 techniques, disengage and launch a new attack.
- If you continually score with a certain technique, keep using it! Force your opponent to make you stop from scoring with a specific attack. In other words, if it is not broken, don't fix it!
- Stay in control of the match. It is your fight; don't allow the opponent to control the tempo of the match.
- Always monitor your range and adjust accordingly (as required). Know how to effectively bridge the gap.

Be prepared to follow up!

(1.) The competitors face off in an open stance.

(2.) The attacker (right) executes a side kick to his opponent's mid-section but the defender (left) blocks the oncoming kick.

(3.) Without hesitation, the attacker follows up his initial attack with a successful back fist, which scores to the head of his opponent.

Scenario # 2

(1.) The competitors face off in an open stance.

(2.) The attacker (right) executes a side kick to his opponent's mid-section but the defender (left) blocks the oncoming kick.

(3.) In this scenario, the attacker hesitates after missing with his first attack, allowing the defender to score with a counter-attack to the head.

Five Methods of Attack

Bruce Lee categorized offense in five separate categories. Although Bruce Lee's Five Methods of Attack are generally associated with more combative applications, his offensive categorization philosophy can also be applied with great success to point fighting.

Single Direct Attack (SDA)

Straightforward single attack aimed at a specific target with no set-up. This is the most basic type of attack.

- Single Direct Attacks tend to be the most successful from a scoring percentage point of view because they usually occur from a fixed, stable stance.
- Speed and proper timing will increase the success of this type of attack.

BACK FIST ATTACK

ROUND KICK ATTACK

Attack by Combination (ABC):

Uses multiple rapid attacks at various targets with the intention of overwhelming the opponent's defense and scoring. This is the preferred method of the "*Blitzer*" style fighter. Sometimes a single direct attack can turn into an attack by combination because your first attack was unsuccessful and your opponent did not counter (so you just keep attacking).

- Rhythm can play a big role in the success of this approach. Attacks do not always have to occur with the same tempo. They can be varied to further bewilder your opponent.
- Recommendations and examples of good ABC-type attacks with legs, hands and combinations are listed in the grid below:

Examples of Attack by Combination (ABC)

Hand ABC Attacks	Foot ABC Attacks	Combination Foot and Hand Attacks
Back fist, reverse punch	Side kick (to body), round kick (to the head) using the same leg	Double jab, round kick
Back fist, reverse punch, ridge hand strike	Round kick, side kick, ax kick – alternating legs	Side kick, back fist, round kick
Back fist, ridge hand strike	Double round kick, spin side kick – alternating legs	Round kick, back fist, reverse punch
Back fist, hammer fist	Hook kick, round kick side kick – using the same leg	Side kick, round kick, reverse punch
Double jab, ridge hand strike	Front kick (to body), round kick (to head) – using the same leg	Front kick, back fist, reverse punch, ridge hand strike

Example #1 Attack by Combination

Classic Extended Blitzing Style Sport Karate Attack

(1.) The competitors face off in a closed stance.

(2.) The attacker (right) executes a side kick to his opponent's mid-section which safely bridges the gap and places him in punching range.

(3.) He immediately follows up with a back fist to the head.

(4.) This opens his opponent's mid-section and the attacker continues his blitzing attack with a reverse punch to the body.

(5.) The attacker finishes his blitz with a ridge hand strike to the head.

Progressive Indirect Attack (PIA):

This approach simulates an attack to one point zone, which then creates an opening to another point zone, because the opponent blocks or otherwise avoids the first attack (the decoy attack). The sequence is immediately followed up with a second attack to a different point zone (that was previously not available) – for the "*real*" attack. This concept aims to distract your opponent with one attack so the second attack can score on an unprotected point zone (created by the initial attack). You want your opponent to react to your strike. If he doesn't, then this concept can quickly become a Single Direct Attack, as you will have scored with a single technique. Due to human physiology, we cannot protect every potential point area simultaneously and be in range. For example, blocking a high technique will create an opening somewhere on the mid-section. The same is true of blocking a mid-section attack; this will create an opening on the high line.

Example #1 Progressive Indirect Attack

(1.) The competitors face off in a closed stance.

(2.) The attacker (left) steps in and executes a back fist to his opponent's head. The defender (right) blocks the incoming attack.

(3.) The defender's initial block leaves his mid-section wide open and the attacker takes advantage of this opening and delivers a side kick to the body.

(4.) A possible variation is to substitute the side kick with a round kick instead.

Example #2 Progressive Indirect Attack

(1.) The competitors face off in a closed stance.

(2.) The attacker (right) steps in and executes a back fist to his opponent's head. The defender (left) blocks the incoming attack.

(3.) The attacker immediately follows up with a penetrating reverse punch to his opponent's mid-section.

Example #3 Progressive Indirect Attack

(1.) The competitors face off in a closed stance.

(2.) The attacker (left) executes a round kick feint to his opponent's mid-section.

(3.) The attacker re-chambers his kicking leg.

(4.) The defender (right), reacting to the re-chamber, anticipates a follow-up kick to the mid-section and lowers his guard; the attacker takes advantage of the opening and scores with a second round kick to the head.

Attack by Drawing (ABD)

Counter-fighting is another way to describe this method. The goal is to draw your opponent into a committed movement either offensively or defensively by baiting him or her with intentionally exposed targets or specific motions that elicit a response. Once an opponent reacts, he or she is temporarily committed to that reaction and is extremely vulnerable to your counter-attack. Quick interception of your opponent's reaction is critical to make this method produce points for you. Speed, timing and distance awareness are essential.

Example #1 Attack by Drawing

(1.) The competitors face off in an open stance.

(2.) The attacker (right) is baited by his opponent's low guard and executes a rear leg round kick to the mid-section. The defender (right) quickly switches stance and avoids the oncoming kick.

(3.) Before the attacker can reset (and while he is still off balance), the defender follows up and scores with a rear leg round kick to his opponent's body.

Example #2 Attack by Drawing

(1.) The competitors face off in an open stance and the fighter on the right intentionally lowers his guard in an effort to bait his opponent into attacking.

(2.) The fighter on the left executes a rear leg round kick to his opponent's body, but his opponent is prepared for the attack and immediately initiates his counter-attack by hop-spinning away from the kick

(3.) and delivers a jump spin back kick to his opponent's mid-section, which scores.

Example #3 Attack by Drawing

(1.) The competitors face off in an open stance.

(2.) The attacker (right) slides in

(3.) and executes a round kick to his opponent's head, which the defender (left) successfully blocks.

(4.) The attacker recovers from the kick but pretends to be off balance and vulnerable to a punching attack to the head but in reality the attacker is safe because he is balanced, his body is protected by his lead arm and his head is out of range because he is leaning back; the defender instinctually reacts to what he perceives as an easy point by moving in to deliver his reverse punch.

(5.) The attacker delivers a perfectly timed counter-hook kick to his opponent's head before the reverse punch can hit him.

Hand/Foot Immobilization Attack - Attack by Trapping (HIA)

This method utilizes trapping (pinning or grabbing) the opponent's limb(s) while simultaneously following up with short range strike(s) and applying continued backward pressure forcing the opponent onto his or her heels.

Example #1 Hand/Foot Immobilization

(1.) The competitors face off in a closed stance.

(2.) The attacker (right) executes a knife hand block to his opponent's lead hand.

(3.) He follows up by quickly grabbing his opponent's wrist

(4.) and pulls the opponent toward him while simultaneously executing a side kick to the body.

Example #2 Hand/Foot Immobilization

(1.) The competitors face off in a closed stance.

(2.) The attacker (left) steps in and slaps down his opponent's guard while simultaneously forcing his opponent backward and off balance.

(3.) He continues to step through, maintaining downward pressure with his checking hand, and delivers his lead hand vertical punch to the opponent's head.

Example #3 **Hand/Foot Immobilization**

(1.) The competitors face off in a closed stance.

(2.) The attacker (right) executes a reverse punch to his opponent's body. The defender (left) zones out and blocks the oncoming attack with a right outside knife hand block.

(3.) He follows up by quickly grabbing his opponent's wrist

(4.) and pulls the opponent toward him while simultaneously executing a rear leg round kick to the body.

Quick Reference

Offensive techniques applied under the following circumstances have the highest probability of successfully scoring:

- As the opponent advances (or enters).
- As the opponent retreats (or exits).
- In an immediate attack from the *"Begin"* command. Right off the line.
- When your opponent changes his or her stance.
- When your opponent's hand position changes (i.e., dropping his or her hands when kicking, etc.).
- During the opponent's reaction to a feint.
- Immediately after the opponent has missed you (and is still in the act of recovering from the miss).
- When the opponent has stopped moving and has become *"flat footed."*
- When an opponent is off balance or out of position (particularly if he or she is reaching with the attack).

Chapter 11: Defense

Defense is the act of preventing the opponent from scoring while simultaneously working toward your own attack (the nullification of your opponent's offense). Pure defense alone does not work without the immediate ability to toggle into offense and quickly back into defense if necessary. If you just block once or move out of the way, eventually your opponent will score on you. No one can block or evade indefinitely!

Key Factors in Defense

- Good fighters can seamlessly phase in and out of offense or defense as required at any given time during the match.
- Footwork is key in point fighting defense. Be on your toes and bounce as much as possible. Make your opponent miss and then immediately counter. In point sparring, the *"Evade and Hit"* strategy is generally preferable to the *"Block and Hit"* strategy.
- Blocking is more than a single dimensional response. Blocks can also be strikes! Soft blocks can redirect and open up counter-scoring possibilities. Blocking capabilities are also improved through good footwork.
- Remember, if you are close enough to block, you are close enough to hit (and be hit).
- Simultaneous block-strike combinations are more effective than blocking and striking in separate motions.
- Off-angling (or zoning out) is an efficient way of making an opponent miss, while leaving you in the best counter-scoring position.
- Stop-hit combos disrupt the attack flow and offer quick opportunities for fast follow-up techniques.

Natural Nullifying Techniques

For every technique, there is a counter-technique. Successful competitors understand on a very basic level how techniques complement each other, and especially how certain techniques have a natural nullifying effect against others. These can be broken down into two primary methods:

1. Static Counter-Response (SCR)

Some techniques, by very their design, will immediately cancel out other techniques without the need for evasive footwork and can be delivered in place directly from the fighting stance. The defender just needs to properly time the execution of the counter-technique.

2. Dynamic Counter-Response (DCR)

Other techniques require some form of initial footwork or movement, usually a simple side step or stance switch, prior to delivering the counter-kick. This type of counter must be done smoothly and quickly to ensure that the window of opportunity is fully realized. The dynamic counter-response requires only enough initial movement to make your opponent miss. Moving too far out of position will prevent your opponent's attack from scoring, but it will also take you out of range to counter. Dynamic counter-responses also require timing such that the actual counter-technique is fired before your opponent can recover from his initial attack.

Examples of SCR and DCR responses

A static counter response to a rear leg round kick to the body.

(1.) From an open stance, your opponent (left) executes a rear leg round kick to your mid-section.

(2.) The static counter-response would be to execute a spinning back kick to your opponent's body. The act of spinning away from the kick protects you from being scored upon because you are moving in the same direction as the oncoming kick. At the same time, you are presenting your opponent with an illegal target area (your back). Having spun away, you now have an open target on the opponent's opposite side.

(3.) Done quickly enough, you will not only avoid the oncoming kick, but also have the option of delivering the spin side kick to an unprotected point area while your opponent is on one leg and either recovering (re-chambering his kicking leg) or still in the process of attacking. Either way, you basically have a free shot on a momentarily vulnerable opponent.

A Static Counter-Response to a Rear Leg Round Kick to the Head

(1.) The competitors face off in an open stance.

(2.) The attacker (left) attempts a rear leg round kick to his opponent's head – but the defender (right) avoids the attack by spinning away and simultaneously begins to set up his counter-kicking technique.

(3.) The defender completes his counter-kick and scores with a spinning hook kick to the head.

A Dynamic Counter-Response against a Front Leg Round Kick

(1.) *The competitors face off in a closed stance.*

(2.) *The attacker (left) initiates an attack with a rear leg front kick, which causes the defender (right) to respond by off angling to avoid the technique.*

(3.) *Once clear, the defender counters with a round kick to the head.*

There are many counter-kicking possibilities, some of which are listed below:

Quick Reference Counter-Kicking Chart

Stance	Attacking Technique	Target	Response Type	Counter Technique	Target
Open	Rear leg round kick	Body	SCR	Spin side kick	Body
Open	Rear leg round kick	Head	SCR	Spin hook kick	Head
Closed	Rear leg round kick	Head	SCR	Lead leg hook kick	Head
Closed	Rear leg hook kick	Head	DCR	Lead leg side kick	Body
Open	Rear leg hook kick	Head	DCR	Rear leg inside ax kick	Head
Open	Lead leg side kick	Body	DCR	Rear leg hook kick	Head
Closed	Lead leg side kick	Body	DCR	Rear leg outside ax kick	Head
Open	Rear leg ax kick	Head	SCR	Spin side kick	Body
Closed	Rear leg ax kick	Head	DCR	Lead leg side kick	Body
Open	Reverse punch	Head or Body	SCR	Lead leg side kick	Body
Closed	Reverse punch	Head or Body	SCR	Lead leg side kick	Body
Open	Back fist	Head	SCR	Lead leg side kick	Body
Closed	Back fist	Head	SCR	Lead leg side kick	Body
Closed	Rear leg front kick	Body	DCR	Rear leg round kick	Head
Open	Rear leg front kick	Body	DCR	Rear leg round kick	Head
Open	Spin side kick	Body	DCR	Rear leg inside ax kick	Head
Closed	Spin side kick	Body	DCR	Lead leg side kick	Body
Closed	Rear leg side kick	Body	DCR	Rear leg outside crescent kick	Head
Open	Rear leg side kick	Body	SCR	Spin hook kick	Head
Closed	Lead leg round kick	Head	SCR	Lead leg round kick	Body
Open	Lead leg round kick	Head	SCR	Rear leg round kick	Body
Closed	Rear leg inside ax kick	Head	SCR	Lead leg front kick	Body
Open	Rear leg inside ax kick	Head	SCR	Lead leg front kick	Body

SCR= Static Counter-Response
DCR= Dynamic Counter-Response

IMPORTANT NOTE: A SIDE KICK CAN BE USED AS A NULLIFER IN NEARLY ANY SITUATION (both in SCR and DCR situations)!

Quick Reference

If defensive concepts are to be effective in sparring, they must include the ability to quickly toggle to offense. Pure defense alone cannot win a match. When defense is applied under the following circumstances it has the highest probability of success:

- When the opponent incorrectly exceeds range and is out of position.
- Between the opponent's attacks (timing is critical here).
- Before the opponent completes his or her attack.
- As the opponent ceases the attack (because he thinks he scored or is throwing single direct attacks).
- As the opponent retreats (on the way out).

Chapter 12:
Types of Fighters and How to Defeat Them

There are several types of sparring philosophies in Sport Karate. A number of factors influence a fighter's approach including his or her physical characteristics, skill and confidence level, fighting preferences and overall cardiovascular fitness. There are three basic point fighting approaches or styles. A fighter may predominately fight using one approach most of the time or may exhibit characteristics from the other types as circumstances dictate. It is most important to first understand these three types of fighters and develop strategies to beat them, and to realize that a fighter is not bound to any one of them and may, in fact, change his or her approach during the course of a match.

Runners

Runners are fighters who seem to be in a constant state of defense. They dance around most of the fight and when attacked, move completely away and out of range of counter-attack (by them) and follow-up (by you). You may sometimes feel that you are chasing these fighters more than actually fighting them.

Blitzers

Blitzers are aggressive, "*in-your-face*" type of fighters who constantly drive forward while delivering a flurry of attacks as they move in. They use intimidation as a tool; if not handled correctly, a blitzer can end the match quickly.

Counter-fighters

True Counter-fighters are arguably the most difficult opponents to spar. They are very patient and possess excellent timing and critical distance point awareness. They will wait for you to make a mistake, and then quickly exploit it through counter-attack. Good Counter-fighters exert little energy chasing you around the ring and only execute techniques when they think they can score. They are very similar to a sniper who waits patiently for a target to present itself and then takes a single, successful shot.

Basic Strategies Against Different Opponent Types

Against the "Runner"

- Runners need to be corralled. Trap them in the corner of the ring using your footwork. Once in a corner, a Runner is contained and easier to score upon.
- Through misdirection, you can control where the Runner *"runs."* This can be accomplished by using a series of linked techniques. The first technique is a feint, designed to force your opponent to *"show his hand"* and *"run"* to a predictable area of the ring. In this example (shown on the right) the attacker lifts his leg to simulate a kicking attack. The defender reacts by moving away from the kick. The second movement is the real attack, set up by the first decoy movement and executed to where you forced attacker. The attacker executes a back fist to the opponent's head before he has time to complete his initial movement. The defender literally runs into the punch. It is important not to over commit on your initial attack or you risk being out of position to deliver the follow-up attack. Basically, your first technique sets up your second technique. It is the second technique (by design) that ultimately scores.

Shuffle Kick to Counter the Runner

- Shuffle kick to confuse a Runner's timing. Most runners move using long steps. The longer the steps are, the more time it takes to complete them. Shuffle kicking requires an initial short quick step followed by your actual kick. A Runner's reaction to your initial shuffle (or short step) makes this work because he will react with a long step backward, which essentially takes more time than your entire shuffle kick sequence. While the Runner is retreating, you know where your opponent is heading as well as the appropriate distance necessary to hit him before his retreat is complete. In essence, your short step initiates your opponent's longer retreating step and before he can complete it, you have already launched your second, more committed attack. Since your opponent has not had a chance to complete the initial retreating motion, he cannot adjust to your second attack in enough time to avoid being hit.

Against the "Blitzer"

- Shut a Blitzer down as early as possible before he gains too much forward momentum. You need to immediately take the fight to him. Be decisive and use the strongest most direct techniques in your arsenal. Hesitation benefits the Blitzer.
- Don't allow a Blitzer to run you straight back (*more than two steps*). Use off angling to defuse the blitz and immediately counter before your opponent has time to recover (i.e., gain balance, put foot down, etc.). This causes the Blitzer to constantly re-adjust for every miss, giving you ample opportunities for counter-scoring.

Shutting Down a Blitzer

Shut the Blitzer down as quickly as possible!

(1.) The competitors face off in a closed stance.

(2.) The attacker (left) blitzes in with a back fist to his opponent's head but the defender (right) immediately responds with a side kick to the mid-section, which momentarily halts the attack.

(3.) As the attacker prepares an immediate follow-up to his initial attack with a reverse punch, the defender re-chambers his initial kick.

(4.) As the defender begins to launch his follow-up reverse punch, the defender beats him to the point with a jump spinning side kick to the body.

Against the "Counter-Fighter"

- Vary your techniques. Using the same combination(s) consistently results in the Counter-fighter easily finding an opening and scoring. Varying your movements makes it harder to read and counter your technique.
- Feinting works well against the Counter-fighter, but needs to be convincing enough for the Counter-fighter to react. Once you know what he is doing you can react accordingly. This approach is essentially to *"counter the Counter-fighter."*
- Practice unorthodox delivery of your techniques. Textbook techniques look great in the forms division but they tend to be easily recognized and easily telegraphed. Bill *"Superfoot"* Wallace made a career out of making his three main kicking techniques look identical from the chamber, making it harder to know exactly what was coming next (and more challenging to Counter-fighters).

Beyond the basic three types of fighters in Sport Karate, you should also take into account the attributes or physical characteristics of any fighter you may face. The following are other factors to consider when devising your overall point sparring strategy.

Against the Kicking Specialist

- Even the best kickers have to put their foot down at some point (what goes up must come down). When they do, move in and attack. This must be properly timed, as your opportunity will only last a fraction of a second. Your counter-attack must be coordinated with the exact moment the opponent places his or her foot down (before regaining balance). If you wait too long, the opponent will have a chance to re-chamber the leg and launch another attack.
- Against kickers, off-angle and attack. Off-angle to get inside the kicker's range and counter with hand techniques.
- Lateral footwork is preferred for dealing with kickers, as it forces them to constantly readjust their attack. This takes effort and time, presenting you with the opportunity for effective counter-striking. It is also much harder to modify the attack to match your defensive movement. Vertical footwork should be avoided because it is too easy to misjudge the critical distance point. Kickers can adjust the penetration of their kicking attack much easier on a vertical plane.
- Jamming a kicker effectively takes the kicker out of range and presents you with a counter-attack opportunity.

Against the Puncher (Hand Technique Specialist)

- Don't allow the puncher the chance to set up. Keep moving, using circling footwork. Use your lead leg kicks to disrupt and keep your opponent out of punching range. Look for an opening and apply a counter-technique! Timing is critical here!
- If the opponent manages to establish successful combinations, do not allow him to run you straight back. Off-angle and counter-attack!
- Keep your distance. If possible, keep the puncher in kicking range where he cannot reach you.

Against Shorter Opponents

- Use long weapons (kicks) to keep them out of scoring range.
- Use noncommittal lead leg kicks, such as the round kick, to *"jab"* at your opponent, keeping him outside while you look for a solid scoring opportunity. You need to be bouncing and not stationary. Footwork is very important here.

Against Taller Opponents

- Much like a kicker, you need to off-angle and launch immediate counter-strikes while they are *"resetting"* from their missed attack. Blitz-style attacks are desirable against this type of opponent.
- Close the gap through good circling footwork. This will help get you safely inside range and negate their height advantage.

Against Slower Opponents

- Keep it simple (use the fundamentals).
- Make them come to you. Don't chase after them.
- Counter-fighting techniques tend to be more effective on slower opponents.
- Do not underestimate them. Very often a slower opponent can affect the overall tempo of a fight in his or her favor.

Against Faster Opponents

*** This is a useful strategy for older fighters against younger opponents or even as a possible backup strategy for tired or injured fighters.**

- Keep covered and stay in position. Present them with as few scoring opportunities as possible.
- Conserve energy. Remember, kicking and punching even when you miss takes a great amount of energy.
- Let your opponent commit to an attack while you shield it and simultaneously penetrate into his or her range with low risk/high percentage type of counter-techniques such as reverse punch or front kick.
- Keep tight and do not chase techniques with blocks. Patience is key.
- Maintain distance whenever possible. The greater the distance you put between you and your opponent, the more time you have to react to his attacks.

(1.) The competitors face off in an open stance.

(2.) The attacker (left) executes a quick penetrating jab to the head but the defender (right) counters by "sitting" down in his stance while simultaneously blocking and delivering a reverse punch to the body. Because the attacker is committed to his jab he cannot stop the momentum of his attack in time to avoid literally running into the defender's punch.

Chapter 13: Common Sparring Mistakes

- Executing techniques when you are out of range. This leaves you susceptible to counter-attack and wastes energy.
- Blocking with two hands. This is a fairly common mistake with new competitors that should be avoided, as it creates a major opening for counter-attack.
- Too much withdraw, or moving too far out of range to avoid being hit. Doing this leaves you little chance to counter.
- Lack of footwork.
- Random hitting. You should pick your targets and don't use the *"swing and pray"* approach.
- Excessive lag time between hits.
- Reaching for blocks. This draws you out of position and makes counter-attacking much easier for your opponent. Whenever possible, use footwork to avoid (just get out of the way).
- Lack of techniques. Concentrating on a handful of proven techniques is recommended, but you must have enough to keep your opponent guessing and should always have contingency techniques in reserve in case your primary techniques fail to produce points.
- Excessive lag time between block and counter-technique. Point fighting is a very fast game where your opportunity to counter is measured in tenths of seconds.
- Directly attacking an entrenched fighter when the opponent is *"ready."* First draw him or her out of position with angled attacks or feints.
- Inability to control your emotions. Never allow your opponent to know you are hurt, frustrated or scared.
- Inappropriate distance: too close or too far to properly execute your attack.
- Hesitation.
- Posing after an attack. You are in a sparring match, not a photo shoot!
- Stopping after you think you scored. You should only stop after the officials issue the *"break"* command.
- Not following up.
- Lack of commitment or wishy-washy technique.
- Not properly setting before you execute your power techniques.
- Not enough moving around (being too stationary).
- Dropping your guard when you attack.

- Bad mechanics, bad body alignment.
- Trying to use every technique you ever learned in one match. Balance between what works for you while still presenting enough to keep your opponent guessing.
- Pulling your shots short of contact.
- Unnecessary movement — it wastes precious energy (this includes missing).
- Overusing feints.
- Overuse of jumping or spinning techniques. If a more basic technique will work, it should be used instead.
- Thinking you can win every match. This is simply not possible.
- Standing toe-to-toe and trading blows.
- Not having a game plan. You must have a strategy going into a match.
- Trying too hard to win.
- Failure to use explosive movements in both offense and defense. Such movements help get you there first.
- Not adjusting properly to your opponent. If you throw three round kicks and they don't score, DON'T throw a fourth; instead change the attack. Not adjusting makes you predictable and extremely susceptible to counter-attack. The opposite is also true — if you are successfully executing the same technique, don't stop until your opponent stops you.
- Not using enough footwork, or using bad footwork.
- Not having fun.

Chapter 14:
Sparring Drills

Side Press Block/Back Fist Drill

This drill is designed to increase your ability to block and counter with greater speed and accuracy against the back fist, the most common hand attack in the sport. It also is an excellent way to help break the *"flinch tendency"* common to most new point fighters by exposing them to repeated (but controlled) attacks to the head. This drill requires two people wearing sparring gear. Both fighters face each other in fighting stances (using the low guard hand positioning) in punching range. The drill starts with Fighter 1 launching a back fist toward the head of Fighter 2. Light-to-moderate contact should be used. Fighter 2 immediately executes a side pressing block to deflect the oncoming back fist and immediately counters with a back fist of his or her own (toward the head of Fighter 1). Do not overextend the pressing block or you will leave yourself open to an easy counter-attack possibility. Fighter 1 then side press blocks the oncoming back fist followed by a counter-back fist to the head of Fighter 2. These actions are repeated for the duration of the drill, recommended at 1 to 3 minutes per round. This drill should resemble a ping pong game with the action moving back and forth (each participant takes a turn throwing a back fist).

Fighter 1

Fighter 2

Pump Kicking

This is a method of delivering a series of quick, multiple lead leg round kicks that are repeatedly chambered, fired and re-chambered without putting the foot down between kicks. Pump kicking can sometimes utilize footwork such as hopping or sliding toward the target to enhance its effectiveness and to stay within range of the intended target. Pump kicking requires a fighter to possess exceptional balance, body mechanics, flexibility and strength. The key factor in pump kicking is returning to the chambered position after each kick and then immediately executing the next kick, without putting the foot down. Pump kicking can be used as a drill (outside of sparring) to improve your ability to use tournament style round kicks in competition. It can also be used in actual point sparring engagements as a form of offense. Pump kicking is not intended to be power based in nature; in fact, using too much power (or commitment) is detrimental to this concept because too much power invariably throws the kicker off-balance, making it necessary for him to put his foot down to re-establish balance. Pump kicking needs to be a fast, controlled flurry of attacks that is not fully committed. Pump kicking should be drilled regularly. Begin by launching a single round kick then place the foot back on the floor (returning to a fighting stance). Next, launch two round kicks in rapid secession, and again return the foot to the floor. Try adding a kick to each set until you max out. Another approach is doing as many pump kicks as you can over a timed period, usually 30 to 60 seconds.

Quick Draw Kicking Drill

This reaction drill requires three people: two to actively participate and the other to call "*draw*" or "*go*." Both partners face off against one another in a closed fighting stance. It is imperative that they are within kicking range. The third person then calls "*draw*" or "*go*." Each fighter will immediately throw one round kick at the other (to the head). The fighter who scores first wins that set. This exercise can be done with two fighters (or within a larger group) and can even be used in line sparring (see page 145) . The main goal of this drill is to develop a quicker reaction time while improving the chamber height of your round kick. Generally, the person who can chamber his kicking leg the quickest (and the highest) will score first. The other will fail to score because his leg, being lower than the opponent, will be deflected down and away. This drill can be done in as many sets with as many reps per set as you see fit. For added fun, try making the sets and reps an odd number, so somebody can "*win*" each time. It is important to note that when working this drill, under-kicking can sometimes occur. The best way to prepare for under-kicking is by using a protective groin cup.

Pad Reaction Drill

Pad reaction drills utilize focus pads to help develop both the fighter's reaction time and technique accuracy. Working focus pad drills requires a minimum of two participants: one to hold the pads (a coach) and one to hit them (the athlete). This drill can be conducted in a static mode, where the athlete stays in place and punches and kicks on cue. It can also be applied more dynamically, where the athlete applies a *"blitzing style"* attack using sliding, skipping or jumping footwork to enter as he punches or kicks. While both methods are beneficial, the approach that best prepares the athlete for point fighting competition involves the blitzing style approach. Beginners generally start off using a single pad, and as they improve, a second pad can be introduced. Eventually, two pads are presented with the expectation that two attacks will be delivered at once (or within micro seconds of one another). First, designate the techniques that will be used in the drills. Common techniques include a back fist and reverse punch. Next, identify the relationship between how the pad is held and what technique is expected. For example, a pad held sideways facing toward the fighter at head level would indicate a back fist. A pad held in a similar manner but body level would indicate a reverse punch. Begin in a fighting stance, with the holder standing in front of you. At first, the holder may leave the targets out there (in a static manner) allowing for easier technique identification. The athlete (using footwork) moves in and strikes the pads with the appropriate technique (depending on the position of the pad). The techniques should bring the athlete past the pads and the holder. The athlete will immediately turn (changing direction) and move toward the pad again, this time using the opposite lead to ensure more balance in the training. It is important that the athlete get into the habit of *"covering"* after delivering techniques, as good counter-fighters will exploit fighters who don't. As the athlete gains proficiency, the coach can delay presenting the targets, waiting to feed them at the last possible second as the athlete makes his approach. This will shorten the amount of time the athlete has to react and makes the drill more challenging. The coach can randomly feed the pads to develop better reaction for the athlete. For best results, try adding combinations of kicking and hand striking techniques to your pad reaction drills.

Drill #1 Back Fist Blitz

Drill #2 Back Fist-Reverse Punch Blitz

Defense Side Kick Drill

This drill is designed to improve the fighter's ability to properly time and execute a defensive side kick against an approaching opponent. It is considered a reaction drill that enhances critical distance point awareness, balance and overall fighting rhythm. This drill requires two participants and one air shield. One person will hold an air shield tightly against his or her mid-section and simulate an attack by stepping toward the second participant, who will try to keep the opponent away with a defensive side kick. For classification purposes, we will refer to the holder as "*coach*" and the kicker as "*athlete*." The athlete should be delivering a side kick to the opponent's mid-section. The goal for the athlete is to learn to properly time the side kick so that it hits the incoming opponent, neutralizing both the forward progress of the attack while maintaining balance and proper distance in the process. In competition, a successfully delivered defensive side kick generally shuts down the attack and results in a point. If timed incorrectly, the opponent may penetrate into the defender's range, jamming the kick, leaving the defender off-balance and easily scoring in the process. Once the defender can routinely maintain balance after the kick, he can begin to increase the difficulty level of the drill by adding footwork (both participants should be bouncing around), increasing the speed of the simulated incoming attack and reacting to elements of feinting (by the coach).

Defensive Side Kick Drill

Feint variation

(for more experienced competitors)

To better simulate sparring conditions, the holder can feint approaching movement toward the defender in an effort to disrupt his rhythm.

Back kick variation

This variation is identical to the side kick method except the athlete uses a back kick instead.

Line Sparring

Line sparring is a controlled drill used to improve overall sparring skills. It requires a minimum of four fighters and one instructor/coach but ideally should involve eight or more participants. The main benefit of line sparring is it allows the competitor to experience a wider array of opponents of different size, skill level and fighting strategy. To conduct line sparring, competitors form two lines (participants should be wearing appropriate sparring gear); one is line "A" and the other "B." The competitors in each line face each other in ready stances until the instructor/coach issues the command to begin sparring. A normal round lasts 1 or 2 minutes. The instructor/coach signals when time has expired and the competitors return to ready stances again facing each other in two lines. Allow a 1-minute break between each round. Next, have the competitor at the end of one line move to the front; this will allow each competitor to face a new sparring partner when the next round commences. Conduct as many rounds as the competitors' endurance allows, or stop after everyone in line "A" has sparred with everyone in line "B." If there are an odd number of competitors in one line, simply give one a "*bye*" for a round. Line sparring should begin in slow motion and should never exceed medium speed and light contact. This allows the participants to develop proper fighting techniques and gives them an opportunity to experiment. Many times during full-speed sparring sessions, fighters will use only basic (or familiar) techniques and will not attempt more difficult maneuvers for fear of failing or being scored on by an opponent. By line sparring at a slower pace, students can attempt more difficult techniques without fear of being leveled by their opponent. Points should never be awarded for line sparring sessions. Doing so tends to make the drill too competitive, creates a poor training environment and ultimately undermines the purpose of the drill.

Row B
Row A
Row B
Row A

(1.) Students face off.

(2.) Bow to each other to signify the start of the round.

(3.) Assume a ready stance.

(4.) Assume a fighting stance.

(5.) Begin to line spar.

(6.) Return to attention stance.

(7.) Bow to each other to signify the end of the round

(8.) Shift one person down in row B (to create new matchup)

(9.) Students face off.

Press Block/Reverse Punch Drill

This drill is designed to increase the fighter's ability to block and counter with greater speed and accuracy against one of the more common hand attacks in the sport, the reverse punch. Much like the Side Press Block/Back Fist Drill, this drill helps to break a newer fighter's natural tendency to flinch by exposing him or her to repeated but controlled attacks to the head, face and body. This drill requires two people wearing sparring gear. Both fighters face each other in fighting stances in punching range. The drill starts with Fighter 1 playing the role of "*attacker*" by executing a reverse punch to the head or the body of Fighter 2, who plays the role of "*defender*." Light-to-moderate contact should be used in this drill. Fighter 2 immediately executes a downward pressing block with the front hand to deflect the oncoming reverse punch and immediately counters with a reverse punch (toward the head or body of Fighter 1). The reverse punch should be delivered with penetrating footwork (not just thrown from a static position). Care should be taken by the "*defender*" not to overextend on the pressing block because that would leave him out of position and open to counter-attack. The fighters should practice in sets of 10 or 20 attacks in which Fighter 1 attacks and Fighter 2 defends. Timed rounds ranging from 1 to 3 minutes can also be used. Once the desired number of sets is completed, the roles reverse.

Fighter 1 Fighter 2

Counter Kicking Partner Drill

This drill is designed to develop better speed and timing in counter-kicks. It requires two people wearing sparring gear. Both fighters face each other in a fighting stance in kicking range. The drill starts with Fighter 1 executing a lead leg round kick to the body of Fighter 2. Light-to-moderate contact should be used. Fighter 2 takes the hit and the moment Fighter 1's kicking foot hits the floor, Fighter 2 immediately fires back a lead leg round kick to the body of Fighter 1. Timing is essential in this drill! Fighter 1 then quickly fires back a lead leg round kick to Fighter 2's body. The fighters will volley in this manner for the duration of the drill. The recommended time for this drill is 1 to 3 minutes per round. It is essential that the participants take turns kicking each other and resist the urge to throw more than one kick per volley. The tempo of this drill should constantly change from fast to slow, slow to fast, to simulate a sparring match.

Fighter 1 Fighter 2

Variation

This drill can also be done using a free-standing heavy bag. This variation is especially useful for children or for those who lack the ability to physically control the power in their techniques. In this variation, a free-standing heavy bag is placed between both fighters and instead of the fighters actually hitting each other, they hit the heavy bag. The same volley and tempo levels are applied; the fighters are simply hitting the bag instead of each other. It is important that the fighters can see one another over the heavy bag, so make sure the bag is not raised too high.

Critical Distance Awareness Drill

The purpose of this drill is to improve critical distance awareness. This drill requires two participants and a short stick (approximately 28" in length). One participant will swing the stick (the attacker) and the other will avoid being hit. The goal is to avoid being hit by the stick while at the same time not getting so far out of range that a quick counter-attack becomes impossible. The critical distance point is never fixed; rather, it is in a constant state of change. The drill begins with the fighters facing each other just outside kicking range (or just outside the critical distance point). The attacker will step in and swing the stick at the opponent's body. The opponent, through use of footwork and body mechanics, will attempt to avoid the oncoming strike. If the defender can successfully avoid being hit, he immediately tries to get back into range to touch his opponent's shoulder with a hand before the volley is over. This simulates a successful counter-attack by the defender. At first, it will be easier to just avoid being hit and harder to get back into the correct range successfully. That's the challenge of this drill — making the attacker miss by just enough to allow the defender to quickly get back into range to counter-score. The attacker only gets to swing the stick once (in either direction). If the defender is hit with the stick, he "resets" and begins again. It is only when a defender has successfully avoided the strike that he then tries to get back into range and touch the shoulder of the attacker. The footwork used by both participants should simulate a point sparring match (bouncing, light, fluid and quick). Start slowly at first and gradually increase the speed of the drill. Once the participants are comfortable moving in and out of the critical distance point, they can begin to include actual point sparring counters such as back fist and round house kicks instead of simulating the counter-strike by touching the attacker's shoulder. The participants can also begin to add feints as well as broken rhythm-style attacks to further mimic a sparring match. As familiarity with this drill progresses, the attacker can increase the speed of his swing while remembering to exercise caution when swinging the stick. The use of a rattan or padded stick for this drill is highly recommended! The length of this drill is dependent on the participant's stamina. It is a high energy drill! Recommended duration for beginners is 30 second done in multiple rounds. As proficiency increases, so can the length of a round. Ultimately, 1- to 3-minute rounds should be the goal. To make it more interesting, the participants can award points for successful hits, either by the attacker or the defender.

1st Example of Good Critical Distance Awareness

(1.) Participants face each other.

(2.) The attacker (left) swings the stick toward the defender's (right) shoulder. The defender moves back just enough to avoid being hit while still capable of delivering a meaningful counter-attack (getting back inside within a single step).

(3.) The defender steps back in and tags the attacker's shoulder, signifying that he was able to move outside of the critical distance point just enough to make the attacker miss but not far enough to miss the opportunity to counter-score before the attacker could fire a follow-up attack.

2nd Example of Good Critical Distance Awareness

(1.) Participants face each other.

(2.) The attacker (left) swings the stick toward the defender's (right) shoulder, but this time the defender moves too far off the critical distance point to avoid the initial attack.

(3.) The distance created by the defender's initial movement is too much to safely bridge the gap.

(4.) For illustration purposes, the attacker swings the stick back a second time to demonstrate how the defender would be unable to safely bridge the distance and would be hit trying to get back in.

Critical Distance Sliding Side Kick Drill

This drill requires two participants and is designed to help improve both the offensive and defensive aspects of critical distance point awareness. Begin by having both fighters face off in a fighting stance just outside of kicking range. Fighter 1 will execute a lead leg sliding side kick (to the mid-section) while Fighter 2 attempts to maintain the critical distance point by moving back, away from the incoming kick. Fighter 2 can block the kick as a last resort, but should try to make Fighter 1 miss by properly maintaining the critical distance point. The moment Fighter 1's foot hits the ground, Fighter 2 immediately launches a sliding side kick to Fighter 1's mid-section. Timing is absolutely critical! Fighter 1 must now move back to avoid being hit (blocking only as a last resort). Once Fighter 2's foot hits the floor, Fighter 1 immediately launches another sliding side kick and the process goes back and forth, with exchanges continuing for the duration of the round. The length of a round should be from 30 seconds to 3 minutes (depending on the participants' fitness and experience levels). This drill also works using other types of kicks including round house kick, hook kick, front kick and ax kick. Begin this drill slowly and gradually increase the speed and vary the rhythm. Plan on getting hit (because you will). Try to practice this drill with as many different fighters as possible because the critical distance point will be different for every fighter. Ultimately, the more you work with this drill, the better you will be able to judge distance both on the offense and defense.

Fighter 2 Fighter 1

Chapter 15: Conditioning Exercises for the Point Fighter

Interval Running

To be a successful point fighter your cardiovascular system must be in optimal condition. Interval running is an excellent way to improve your level of cardiovascular conditioning. Interval training involves a burst of high intensity activity (like full sprints) followed by rest or low intensity exercise (like walking). Interval running better mimics the conditions of a fight, in which you are alternating between high intensity activities (kicking and punching) and low intensity activities (circling and recovering). Start off with a workout consisting of a 1-minute sprint and then 4 minutes of walking (a ratio of 1:4). Repeat this cycle a total of 5 times (or 25 total minutes of both sprinting and walking). As your cardiovascular conditioning improves, you can adjust your workout to consist of 2 minutes of sprinting and then 4 minutes of walking (a ratio of 1:2). Repeat this cycle 5 times (or 30 total minutes of both sprinting and walking). You can continue to make your interval running more challenging by eventually adjusting the ratio to 1:1. In this workout, you sprint for 2 minutes, then walk for 2 minutes. Repeat the cycle 5 times (or 20 minutes of both sprinting and walking). Although you are only participating in 20 minutes of training, the 1:1 ratio is more challenging because you are now equally splitting the high intensity and low intensity activities. The examples above illustrate the concept of interval training in general; you can structure your interval training to best suit your needs.

Swing Kicks - Side Leg Raises

This exercise is designed to increase your hip strength, which will improve your kicking ability, particularly for your side kick. Do the leg raises exercise to the height and position you want your actual kick to go when you execute it in sparring. It is important to make sure that your support leg is pivoted properly while you do these. If you are having problems with the proper pivot location of the base foot, try to pre-position it before you begin your sets. At first you may only be able to perform a small number of these and at a lower height than you ultimately want. With time and effort, that number will increase. Active fighters should be doing 50 to 100 leg raises per leg several times a week. Once you can do this, you can add burst-drill training to make the exercise more challenging. Execute 3 to 5 side leg raises as quickly as you can, then wait a few seconds and repeat. Try doing this burst drill training in sets of 5 or 10 and gradually increase the number of sets until you max out.

Elastic Band Training

This is a form of resistance training that utilizes elastic bands to improve sparring attributes.

Application

Elastic band training is a two-person exercise. One person will need to secure the elastic band to ensure there is enough tension on the line. We will refer to this person as the "*coach*." The other person will be the actual participant in the exercise. We will refer to this person as the "*athlete*." The elastic band can also be attached around the athlete's waist while the coach holds the ends of the band and provides adequate tension to the band. When the athlete becomes more comfortable, the coach can try to pull the athlete away from the target while the athlete tries to move toward the target with kicking or hand techniques. The athlete can also practice footwork against the tension of the band without kicking or punching. For a more specific/focused workout, the athlete can attach the band directly to his or her wrist to practice hand striking techniques, or around his or her ankle to practice kicks. Adding elastic band exercises to your training program can improve your speed and power, as well as help you gain more neuromuscular coordination and balance. For point fighting, speed and power are more important than pure strength. Strength is how much force you can generate. Power, on the other hand, is how quickly you can generate that force. Point fighting does not require a fighter to generate maximal force, but instead requires a sub-maximal force to be generated very quickly; in other words, you need to be able to move your body weight through space very quickly.

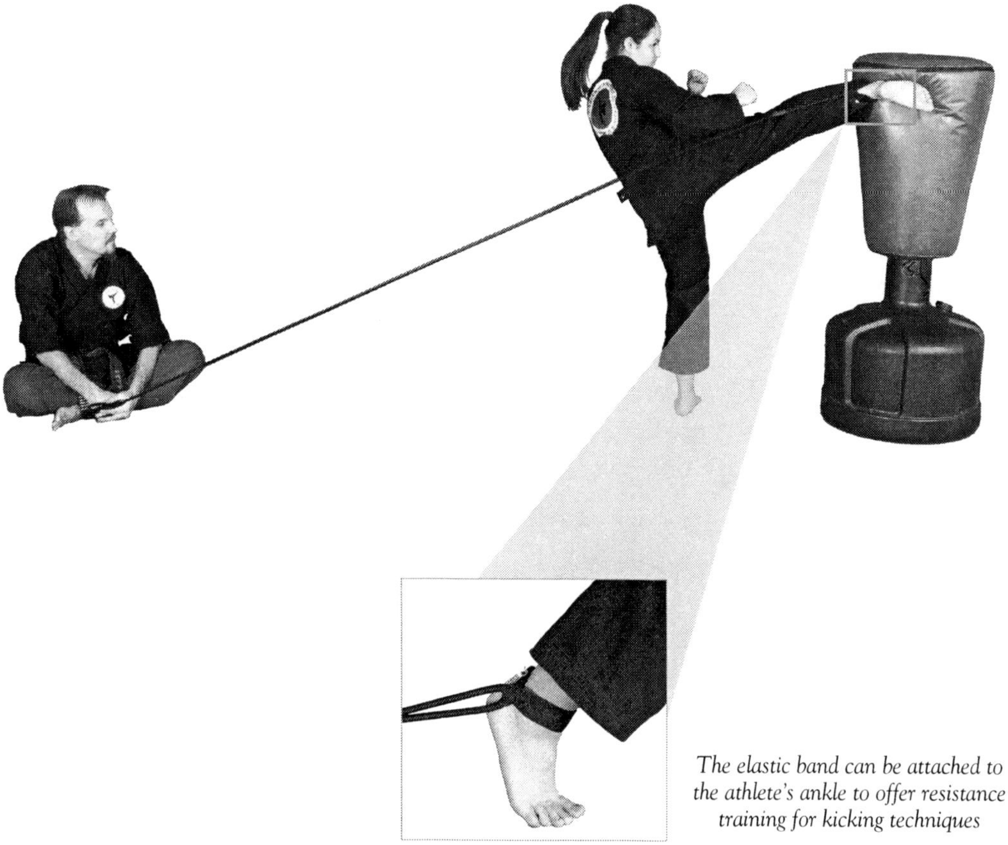

The elastic band can be attached to the athlete's ankle to offer resistance training for kicking techniques

Care should be taken to ensure both ends of the elastic band are properly attached and secured!

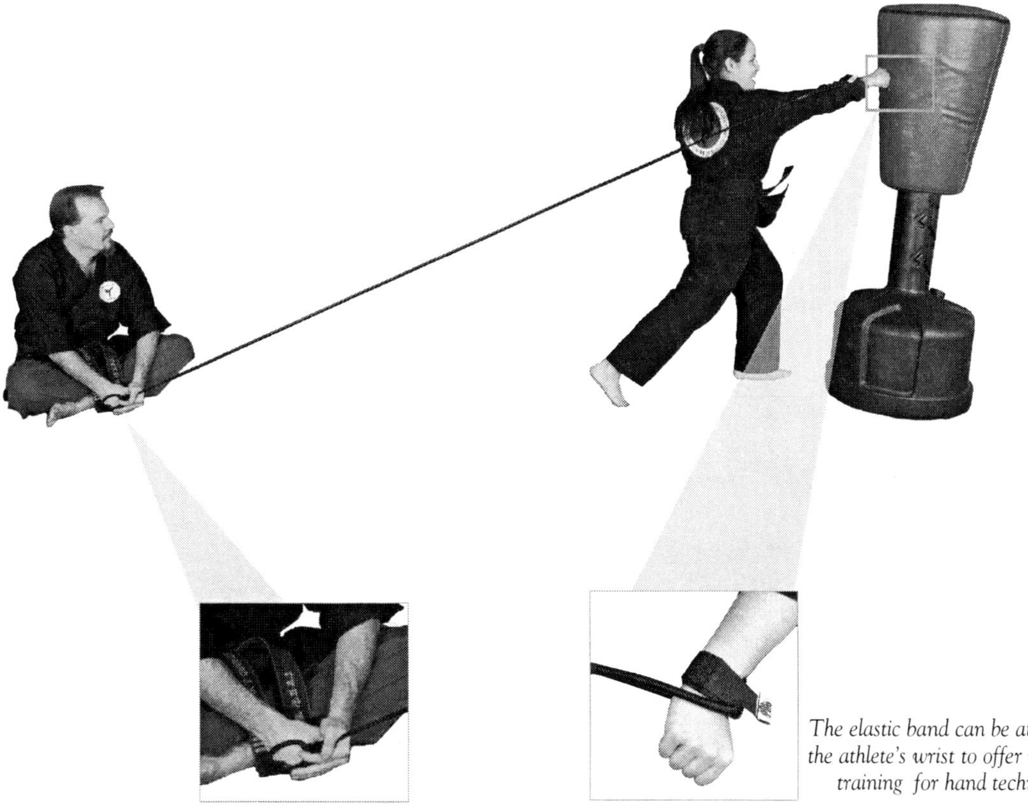

The elastic band can be attached to the athlete's wrist to offer resistance training for hand techniques

Care should be taken to ensure both ends of the elastic band are properly attached and secured!

A Word of Caution

This is an advanced training method that should not be attempted using techniques a fighter is still learning. Even experienced fighters need to start off slowly. Try doing 1 set of 10 reps per leg or arm. Once you are comfortable, you can increase the number of sets and reps. **Stop immediately if you feel any pain!** The holder must properly secure his or her end of the elastic band and verify that the band is properly secured to the kicker before the exercise begins. Routine inspection of the elastic bands is essential to ensure they are safe to use. Discard worn or damaged bands and replace with new ones as needed. The athlete must always perform a thorough warm-up prior to engaging in elastic band training and should only use techniques in which he is proficient. Again, elastic band training is not intended for learning the mechanics of a new technique; rather, it is meant to improve the explosiveness, speed and power of known techniques.

In the examples below, elastic band training can also be more dynamic and free-flowing. This can be done by attaching the band to the athlete's waist, allowing the coach to provide varying degrees of tension the athlete has to work against for a set time period (1- to 2-minute rounds). In this variation,

the athlete is expected to attack the bag with as many hand and foot techniques as possible before the coach pulls her back. The athlete should not stop her attack until the round ends. As the athlete becomes more proficient in this drill, the coach can apply more tension for longer durations during each round.

Plyometric Training

This type of exercise is designed to produce fast, powerful movements and to improve the function of the nervous system, generally for the purpose of improving performance in sports. Plyometric movements, in which a muscle is loaded and then contracted in rapid sequence, use the strength, elasticity and innervation of muscle and surrounding tissues to jump higher, run faster, throw farther or hit harder, depending on the desired training goal. Plyometrics is used to increase the speed or force of muscular contractions, providing explosiveness for a variety of sport-specific activities.*

Plyometric training is a method of power exercises that involves jumping and hopping to utilize the athlete's own body weight to develop explosive power. In point sparring, the ability to explode in and out of offense and defense is essential to be successful in competition. Plyometric exercises include drills such as jumping in place, leaping, bounding and even running and skipping. This training takes advantage of the stretch reflex in the muscles and could be equated to stretching a rubber band and then letting it go. The further you stretch the rubber band, the more rapidly it returns. To illustrate how this works, consider the example of jumping from a flat-footed stance. If you try to leap in the air without first crouching down, you cannot jump very high. If instead you squat down first and then leap in the air, you will jump much higher. Squatting down first stretches the muscles in your thighs before you contract them. As a result, you will be able to generate more force out of them, which typically results in a higher jump. Take it a step further: squat down quickly and immediately jump up, and you will get even higher. This is because the faster you stretch the muscle, the quicker it snaps back, generating more power and allowing you to gain more height.

Plyometric exercises are very demanding because they involve dynamic, high-force movements through a wide range of motion. This type of training should only be undertaken after you establish a significant base of strength and flexibility. Generally, an athlete would want to add these drills after accomplishing a base conditioning program, which includes aerobic training, stretching and also several phases of resistance training. Because of the forces applied to the ligaments and tendons, these exercises are generally not advised for athletes with knee or back problems. And for all athletes, plyometric exercises are best performed on a more forgiving surface. Padded martial arts flooring is good for shock absorption, as are grass and dirt. Avoid performing plyometric exercises on concrete or asphalt surfaces.

* *Wikipedia*. 2010. 9, July, 2010 *<http://en.wikipedia.org/wiki/Plyometrics>*

Examples of Plyometric Exercises for Point Sparring

The following plyometric exercises can be performed in sets or done for specific predetermined time periods. Remember that quality is more important than quantity. As proficiency increases, you can perform the exercises for longer periods of time or in more sets.

Lateral Hurdle Jumps

Foot Bouncing

Burpees

Double Knee Jumps

Clap Push Ups

Chapter 16: How to Increase Fighting Speed

The question of how to increase fighting speed is frequently asked by Sport Karate practitioners. This chapter will outline and discuss some of the strategies and methods that will lead to increasing your fighting speed. The first thing to understand is that fighting speed is much more than the time it takes for your kick or punch to go from point A to point B; anyone with sparring experience knows this. Fighting speed is all about the ability to hit your opponent first. To most effectively do this, you need to examine your overall fighting strategy; you cannot simply train to increase the speed of your kicks or punches in isolation. True fighting speed takes into account not only the speed of the technique but elements such as footwork, timing and spatial awareness. There are no quick, overnight solutions to increasing your fighting speed, only a lot of effort and hard work. The following more common methods to increasing fighting speed for point sparring are intended to work in tandem and not as standalone solutions, as increasing fighting speed requires an integrated approach.

Relax when executing your techniques.

Tension kills speed! Many times fighters will try to "*muscle*" their techniques, especially beginners or frustrated fighters. This is counter-productive on multiple levels: (1.) Excessive contact is illegal in point sparring. (2.) Tensing up the muscles wastes considerable energy and substantially slows down the delivery of the technique. (3.) Tensed or muscled attacks tend to be more telegraphed and easier to detect and counter. (4.) Tensed muscles are more prone to injury. When the attack is thrown from a relaxed state it is much quicker and more effective because a relaxed muscle is a quick muscle!

Work your footwork!

Many fighters, especially beginners, do not realize there is a difference between fighting speed in throwing combinations on the inside of your opponent range, and fighting speed when closing the distance from the outside of the range. Some fighters are able to execute impressive combinations with considerable speed from the inside when their opponent is in range, but struggle when they are out of their opponent's range. If you are fighting from the outside, your punching and kicking speed is limited by the ability of your feet to take you to your target. In other words, if your feet can't get you there fast enough, your punches or kicks will be short no matter how fast you execute them. Time invested in improving footwork is time well spent improving overall fighting speed!

Throw twice the number of kicks or hand strikes that you currently throw per workout.

In order to kick quickly you need to kick a lot. Only through the execution of numerous kicks will your brain effectively communicate to your muscle fibers the correct way to execute a specific kick (or hand strike). This is also referred to as muscle memory. To become more efficient at any given technique you must execute the desired motion thousands of times. Optimally, you want activate the least amount of muscle fibers to execute a given action, and you need the surrounding muscle fibers relaxed so that the necessary fibers can function without restriction. Repetitive, sport-specific movement is the only way to accomplish this. In a nutshell, if you want to kick and punch fast, throw a lot of kicks and punches.

Increase your total number of sparring rounds.

Three sparring sessions a week is a minimum if you are an active competitor preparing for tournament. Sparring is the ultimate method for simulating the competition scenario where speed is paramount. Sparring also improves other essential fighting attributes relating to speed, such as, timing, distance control, reaction time and overall cardiovascular endurance.

Kick and punch as fast as you can when you train.

Imagine running four sets of 40 yard sprints using only 85% of your total capacity. You could probably do that all day and not get very tired. Now imagine if you were to sprint against a runner who is just as fast as you, but who races at 100% of his or her capacity. Your energy level would be quickly depleted as you try to turn up your output capacity to 100% to match your opponent's speed, especially when you are used to running 40 yards at 85%. Every fighter has a unique speed threshold. If you consistently train at 85% of your maximum punching or kicking speed, then you can only expect to effectively punch or kick at 85% of your potential in the match. Too many fighters practice punching and kicking at 85% (or less) capacity in the dojo. When they enter competition when it really counts, they tend to experience battle fatigue because they are executing their techniques beyond their normal speed threshold. To combat this, successful fighters constantly try to expand (or at the very least maintain) their speed thresholds in the dojo.

Proper body mechanics are essential to deliver the fastest technique possible.

Executing a technique correctly cannot be overemphasized. Having "*good technique*" is more than just winning forms divisions or part of a belt testing requirement. A complete attack (or technique) has an initiation, execution and recovery phase. Each phase must be executed correctly to create the greatest amount of speed. During the initiation phase, your body must be stabilized. A misaligned body, flailing arms or legs and bad balance detract from your fighting speed. During the execution phase, make sure that rear leg kicks come from your hips and front leg kicks snap at the knee. For the recovery portion of a technique, it is important to properly re-chamber. If your punch shoots out, it must return along the same path to be most efficient, effective and fast. Failure to execute the re-chambering or recovery portion of any technique results in "*dead leg*" kicks, which are neither fast nor effective for multiple kicking attacks. Proper body mechanics contribute to both better fighting speed and fighting effectiveness. It is more important to learn and practice a kick or punch correctly, even if it first appears to be slower or awkward. With practice, speed and power will improve.

Tabata Training.

Speed is easy in the early moments of a match, but the best fighters are able to maintain fighting speed throughout an entire match and into subsequent matches. One of the best ways to achieve endurance like that is to be in the best cardiovascular shape possible and condition your body to repetitively deliver techniques. For active competitors, a minimum of two speed workouts per week is required. The use of the "*Tabata Method*" is highly recommended and is very effective for improving the endurance required for point fighting. Tabata training (or the Tabata sequence) is where the athlete engages in 20 seconds of ultra intense exercise immediately followed by 10 seconds of rest. This is repeated for four minutes (or 8 cycles). Sprinting hard for 20 seconds then resting for 10 is a great way to utilize the Tabata method. Kicking or punching a heavy bag for 20 seconds then resting 10 (for a set of 8) is another variation. Ultimately, a basic requirement of being a good fighter is the ability to deliver the fastest technique longer into the match than your opponent. When all things are equal, performing at an optimal level further into the competition is what often separates the winners from the losers.

Flexibility Training.

This is the most overlooked aspect of fighting speed. Flexibility is a joint's ability to move through a full range of motion. Flexibility training increases physical performance. A flexible joint can move through a greater range of motion and requires less energy to do so. Kicking and punching require less effort and less energy to deliver. Greater levels of flexibility also decrease resistance in tissue structures; you are therefore less likely to become injured by exceeding the maximum range of the joint during sparring. Injured muscles move less quickly than healthy ones. Flexibility training also increases neuromuscular coordination. Stretching improves the nerve-impulse velocity, or the time it takes an impulse to travel to the brain and back. This helps opposing muscle groups work in synergy, which greatly improves overall fighting speed. Finally, flexibility training improves muscular balance and posture. Stretching can often help realign soft tissue structures and thus reduce the effort it takes to achieve and maintain good fighting positions when you spar. Active competitors should conduct flexibility training three to four days per week.

Chapter 17: Strategy Improvement

Technique Mapping

Technique mapping is a process that helps a fighter develop an effective game plan for sparring by identifying his best attack and defense options in advance and then drilling those options until they become instinctive reactions. Much like in chess, you want to remain several steps ahead of your opponent. Technique mapping allows you to better achieve this. From a strategic standpoint, there are few things worse than throwing your best technique only to have it miss or be blocked or countered and not know what to do next. Not having an immediate (and effective) follow-up technique to deliver the instant your first effort failed will most often result in your opponent quickly counter-scoring. You want to avoid being reduced to randomly throwing techniques and hoping they score. Your goal should be to execute a series of techniques that are highly likely to score. Technique mapping is useful because it is a pre-planning process that enables a fighter to better understand what techniques will work in advance of the fight, allowing for more meaningful initial attacks as well as follow-up attacks. Technique mapping also is helpful in increasing your overall fighting speed. Through this concept you repeatedly expose yourself to situations that require instant analysis (dealing mainly with perception speed). Repeated exposure leads to making your reaction reflexive. A reflex is fast because you do not think about it, and fast is what wins in point fighting.

The Steps

Offensive Aspects of Technique Mapping

The first step in this process is to define as many potential attacks you have available based on your opponent's stance and hand/foot position (in relation to your own). Scoring opportunities change significantly based on something as simple as facing an opponent in an open stance versus a closed stance. A key point to remember is there are a finite number of attacks allowed in Sport Karate. Your attack options are not limitless, which also means your opponent's attack options are also limited.

After establishing all possible techniques (or as many as you can imagine), analyze which of these potential attacks suit you best. Factors should include your ability to adequately execute the technique in a free sparring environment (it makes little sense to include a head level round kick if you can't consistently kick head level); your personal preference toward a technique (Does the technique fit into your approach? Do you like the technique?) and situational circumstances, such as ability to perform while fatigued or injured. This phase of the process should leave the competitor with 5 to 7 optimal techniques for each circumstance. A fighter's "*optimal techniques*" are highly personalized, fluid and specific to that fighter.

After establishing 5 to 7 optimal techniques (for each circumstance), you then need to rank them, beginning with your favorite or most effective technique. This is referred to as creating an "*ordered response*." An ordered response enables immediate follow-up when the primary attack fails to score. With adequate practice/drilling, a competitor can expect to fire off an impressive attack combination that most opponents will not be able to withstand because the attacks flow faster than the defender can anticipate and react to (overload approach).

Defensive Aspects of Technique Mapping

Technique mapping can also be used for defense. Just as there are a finite number of attacks, the same holds true for the number of realistic options in defensive movements. First, you will need to identify the most common attacks and then pre-plan your defensive response accordingly. Most tournament fighters will use only a handful of techniques; this makes preparation a little easier. While anything is technically possible, it's likely you will face a familiar set of common attacks (albeit at different speeds and power levels). Address the likely first and master your response to those, then worry about the less likely or rarer attack possibilities later.

Speed and power of potential attacks should also be a consideration and a condition within the mapping process. For example, you may have mapped a defensive response to a lead leg round kick to the head. However, if the attacker is especially skilled at delivering very fast head level kicks, your mapping process should treat that as a separate form of attack. In that case, you might want to map a response for a "*normal*" speed head level kick and another separate mapping for excessively fast head level kicks. When facing fast kicks, you will need to shut them down at the source as early as possible, so a potential response could be hard straight line attack to the mid-section to disrupt and unbalance.

Examples From Open Stance

In this example the fighter on the right has identified his top 7 attacking techniques against his opponent in a left lead open stance and assigned an ordered response to each technique. Note the use of mainly lead leg techniques in the fighter's ordered response. Lead leg kicks tend to be quicker and less telegraphed compared to their rear leg counterparts. The techniques shown here are the techniques that worked for this particular fighter in a right lead open stance based on his ability and preference.

(1.) Jab to head

(4.) Hook kick to body

(5.) Round kick to head

(2.) Reverse punch to body

(3.) Side kick to body

(6.) Ax kick to head

(7.) Front kick to body

Examples From Closed Stance

In this sequence the fighter has identified his top 7 attacking techniques against an opponent in a right lead closed stance and assigned an ordered response to each technique. Despite the opponent switching his stance, the fighter still leads with his right foot, so he still controls the fight. However, because his opponent's stance has changed to a closed stance, many of the targets that were available from the open stance will no longer be available. This is not a problem because by using the technique mapping process, the fighter knows in advance what his best options are. The use of mainly lead leg techniques in the fighter's ordered response is worth noting again. Lead leg kicks tend to be quicker and less telegraphed compared to their rear leg counterparts.

(1.) Backfist to head

(4.) Hook kick to head

(5.) Front kick to body

(2.) Round kick to body

(3.) Side kick to body

(6.) Jab to head

(7.) Ridge hand strike to head

Sample Technique Mapping Grid

Stance	First Technique	Second Technique	Third Technique	Fourth Technique	Fifth Technique
Open stance left lead	Jab to head	Reverse punch to body	Side kick to mid-section	Ridge hand to body	Hammer fist to head
Open stance right lead	Jab to head	Side kick to mid-section	Round kick to head	Hook kick to mid-section	Rear leg ax kick to upper body
Closed stance left lead	Round kick to mid-section	Side kick to mid-section	Jab to head	Reverse punch to mid-section	Lead leg ax kick to head
Closed stance right lead	Round kick to mid-section	Back fist to head	Reverse punch to mid-section	Side kick to mid-section	Hook kick to head
Transition from stance switch	Round kick to mid-section	Back fist to head	Reverse punch to mid-section	Side kick to mid-section	Hook kick to head

The connections (relationship) between Open and Closed Stance Scoring Opportunities

If an opportunity exist to score with a specific technique on a middle range target in a closed stance then it also exists with the same technique to a high range target from the opposite side (in an open stance) without having to change your lead.

To further illustrate this concept

In this example, (pictured on page 183) from a closed stance, a mid-section right lead round kick to the body scores but from an open stance that same mid-level round kick is illegal. The opportunity still exists to score with a right lead round kick from an open stance – however, it must now be at head level. Understanding this reality will keep you in control of the fight by not allowing your opponent to force you to switch your lead in order to score with a specific technique. Through the technique mapping process, you can account and plan for all possibilities in advance.

Once technique mapping has been completed, there is less uncertainty as to which techniques are theoretically possible for scoring in any given situation. At first, try to identify the more common techniques and map 3 to 5 techniques deep; as you get better, you can include additional attacks and expand your mapping to 5 to 10 (or as many as you can handle). Ultimately, technique mapping requires a competitor to follow a process-style approach when managing his or her arsenal of offensive and defensive techniques, and to this end to create a successful sparring strategy. The competitor can then work toward ensuring this strategy is effective, efficient and continually improved upon.

Points of Interest about Technique Mapping

- Technique mapping enables you to literally remain one step (or more) ahead of your opponent at all times.
- Some techniques work from either a closed or an open stance. For example: the sidekick to the body and jab to the head.
- Often techniques that work in an open stance will work in reverse when in a closed stance. For example: From a closed stance, a round kick to the body is ideal. In an open stance, that kick would hit your opponent's back (and is illegal), but a head level round kick would work.
- Try to deliver head level kicks from the *"blind spot"* position (in other words, approach them from behind). Executing kicks directly at the person's face will most often result in him seeing the technique and blocking or avoiding it.
- Bear in mind right hand/left hand dominance when performing your technique mapping. Some competitors are great with their right leg and not with their left. This fact will impact your mapping options (never use a technique that you have not mastered).
- The most successful point fighters dictate the match! Do not allow your opponent to force you into switching your stance. If you have mapped correctly you will have a strategy from both an open and closed stance.
- Although the process of technique mapping can be as simple or as complex as you want to make it, when in doubt make it as simple and direct as possible.
- Once you have successfully finished the technique mapping process, use Technique Isolation Drills (TID) to transfer your responses into muscle memory.

Technique Isolation Drills (TID)

Technique Isolation Drills, or TID, is a concept designed to help improve a competitor's sparring ability one technique at a time. It does so by initially allowing each fighter to use a single pre-determined technique against the other in each round when sparring. The exact technique(s) used must be made clear to both participants at the beginning of each round. TID training aims to completely isolate the technique and work it exclusively during the round. This allows fighters to become familiar with a specific technique both from an offensive and defensive perspective.

Offensively, the fighter is going through the repetition of delivering a single technique against an uncooperative and unpredictable opponent in a sparring environment (as opposed to the more predictable heavy bag or focus mitt). Practice in this repetitious manner leads to mastery of any given technique in a very practical sense — it can be used to point fight. Defensively, the fighter also sees the same technique repeatedly and develops a strong familiarity with that specific technique. With enough repetition, fighters can develop the ability to identify an incoming technique early into its execution. This is advantageous in learning the appropriate counter-technique or just avoiding being hit by it. You need to fully understand the fundamental mechanics and proper execution of each technique you plan to use before you begin to work TID with a partner.

TID is not intended to incorporate techniques that the practitioner has not fully mastered on a functional level. If you cannot apply the technique properly on a heavy bag or focus mitt, you should not incorporate it into TID training. Instead, continue to develop techniques independently according to the normal methods prescribed by your specific art.

TID Application

TID requires a minimum of two people; however, the more participants the better, because you have a deeper pool of fighters that can be alternated during each round. This will give you a greater variety of different body types, fighting styles, etc., that you may face in tournament. A coach or instructor is highly recommended, especially when working with beginners. Coaches can serve as timekeepers, make sure the drill is safe and under control and ensures that each fighter is using the correctly assigned technique. With more experienced fighters, the role of coach or instructor is not as important and can either be filled by another fighter (maybe the odd man out) or even just between the two participants engaged in the drill.

Before each round, both fighters are assigned a specific technique that will be used for that round. The duration of a round can be anywhere from 1 to 5 minutes. It is best to start off simple. At first, assign the same technique for each fighter, for example, "*Fighter A*" is assigned a back fist with either hand and "*Fighter B*" is also assigned a back fist with either hand. In the earliest stages, fighters are allowed to use only footwork to evade oncoming strikes. Later, they can add blocks. Either way, attacks can only be made with the technique assigned at the beginning of the round. Initially, techniques exchanged during the earliest rounds should be at half-speed and gradually progress each subsequent round until full speed is comfortable for both fighters. The amount of time for this progression depends on the fighters' skill level, experience and mindset.

The Eight Tiers of TID

The TID concept also utilizes the element of progression and can be separated into eight tiers. While these tiers become progressively complex, a fighter does not necessarily need to sequentially pass though all of them to achieve benefits. The first tier alone is a great method for improving your skills.

Tier I

This first tier assigns the same technique to both fighters for the entire round. This can be as simple as a back fist vs. a back fist or as complex as jump spinning hook kick vs. jump spinning hook kick, as long as both fighters are using the same technique versus each other for the duration of the round.

Tier II

The next tier assigns a different single attacking technique to each fighter for each round. The rule here is they must both be either all kicking or all hand strikes. For example, assigning a reverse punch to "*Fighter* A" and a jab to "Fighter B," or a lead leg round kick to "*Fighter* A" and a lead leg side kick to "*Fighter B*." The idea in this tier is to begin mixing it up.

Tier III

This level involves assigning both a single hand and a single foot attack against the same. Here the fighter has more flexibility in his or her options and can attack with either a hand or foot technique. You can also limit the attacks to left side or right side only.

Tier IV

At this level, you begin to assign hand techniques against foot techniques. A common round could include "*Fighter* A" being assigned a back fist and "*Fighter B*" assigned a lead leg round house kick. This can be very challenging, as fighters must now utilize timing, footwork and blocking to bridge the gaps created by hand techniques versus foot techniques (and vice-versa).

Tier V

Here, fighters are assigned a specific single technique to the left and right hand or the left and right foot. These paired techniques are either all hand or all foot in nature. As an example, "*Fighter* A" may be assigned a jab with the left hand and a reverse punch with the right hand; the same can also be assigned to "*Fighter B*"in the same round. This now introduces combinations from either the hands or the feet. A possible foot combination could include left leg round kick and right leg side kick from either the front or the rear leg position. Use your discretion to mix it up based on the fighters' strengths and weaknesses. If a fighter favors his left leg round kick, make him use his left leg for something other than a round kick, such as a side kick. Instead, assign his weaker leg the round kick (in this case his right leg). You could assign the same two techniques but just reverse the legs for each fighter. "*Fighter* A" is assigned a left leg side kick and a right leg round kick. "*Fighter B*" is assigned a left leg round kick and a right leg side kick. Be creative and look to force the less familiar on to the fighter to improve the overall attack potential.

Tier VI

At this level, the fighters are assigned a specific technique for each limb. These can be the same for each fighter or they may be different. Again, it all depends on the individual fighters and what they need to improve. One example of a Tier VI TID assignment could be "*Fighter A*" left hand jab, right hand ridge hand strike, right leg spin side kick and left leg front kick versus "*Fighter B*" left hand jab, right hand ridge hand strike and right leg round kick and left leg spin side kick. At this tier, fighters should be very proficient in the TID concept. The combination of potential striking assignments can be vast.

Tier VII

In Tier VII, fighters are assigned two possible attacking techniques per limb. So a fighter could be assigned a back fist or a reverse punch on the left hand, a ridge hand or hook punch on the right hand, a hook kick or side kick on the right leg and a round kick and an ax kick on the left leg. Again the opponent can be assigned the same set of technique or different ones depending on his or her needs. In some cases, one fighter may be assigned a single technique per limb and the other double techniques per limb.

Tier VIII

In this final tier, one fighter is assigned all foot techniques and the other fighter all hand techniques, or all foot versus all foot, or all hand versus all hand. You can even limit it to all lead leg versus all rear leg or vice-versa.

Additional Considerations

In addition to assigning a specific set of techniques to each fighter per round, you can assign a specific target for each fighter. For example, "*Fighter A*" may be assigned a rear round kick to the head section of his opponent. "*Fighter B*" may also be assigned a lead leg side kick to the body section only. Specifying target zones makes the drill more challenging and also forces fighters out of their comfort zone. Plus, once a target zone has been designated, the fighter can focus on defending a smaller area of his or her body. This makes it more difficult for the attacker because the defender's focus is exclusively on one area; in essence it shrinks the size of the target in favor of the defender. This now allows the defender to concentrate on what the technique looks like coming at the target without having to monitor multiple areas. This helps the fighter become familiar with the assigned attacking technique so it is not a mystery in actual sparring.

Another variation to TID training is to change the assigned attacks through various stages of the round. For example, for the first half of the round, "*Fighter A*" is assigned lead leg round kicks and "*Fighter B*" is assigned back fist. In the second half of the round, "*Fighter A*" changes his attack technique to the back fist and "*Fighter B*"changes his to lead leg round kicks. This change can occur every minute, if desired. It is imperative that both fighters understand their assignments before entering into the round. To signify the change in the attacking technique, the coach or instructor can simply shout out "*change*" or "*switch*," or use a whistle or buzzer.

Benefits

Improves your Defense

In the initial phases of TID training, a fighter is presented with a single attacking technique against which he must defend. This gives the fighter the opportunity to focus on a single defense instead of worrying about multiple defenses that are typically required during normal sparring. Through prolonged TID training, the fighter gains a greater level of familiarity against a number of single attacking techniques. When a fighter reaches that level, i.e., knowing the angles of delivery as well as the other intricacies about the execution of the technique, he can identify it much earlier and adjust to it quicker, almost like a reflex reaction. This creates a greater chance of shutting it down either though avoidance or counter-attack before it hits him. Given enough time, TID training will allow the fighter to isolate and identify many, if not all, attacking techniques at real-time speed that may come from opponents during a point fighting match.

Improves your Offense

From an offensive perspective, TID develops a fighter's offensive striking tools on a moving and unpredictable target. Unlike striking into the air or hitting a heavy bag, it involves a live opponent who is purposely trying to avoid your attack. Much like with the defensive benefits of TID training, isolating and repeatedly executing a single offensive technique gives the fighter a better feel for it. And with the opponent knowing he is only allowed to attack with that single pre-determined technique, the fighter must utilize better footwork, timing and feinting to be sure of hitting him. With enough practice, the fighter will truly "*own*" the technique, as he will be better able to apply it from a wider range of situations and more effectively as well.

Forces to Train Weakness as well as Strengths

TID training can also force a fighter to train not only his or her strengths but also his or her weaknesses. Most fighters tend to favor certain techniques and, as a result, they use them more often during sparring; they are comfortable and have mastered a specific subset of offensive techniques. To attempt a technique outside of that subset would be unfamiliar or perhaps even awkward. TID training can force a fighter to use techniques he is less familiar with in an effort to improve them. Through isolating the less familiar technique and repetitiously drilling it, the technique becomes more familiar and more likely to be used successfully in an actual fight. In time, the previously less preferred technique may eventually make the fighter's "*A list*" of techniques.

Instantly Creates a Better Pool of Potential Training Partners

Sometimes, the pool of evenly matched fighters may be small at any given training session or class. There may be a number of under-Black Belts and Black Belt fighters grouped together in one training session. At times, the experience level could be mismatched such that Black Belts end up *"holding back"* when sparring non-Black Belts. Utilizing TID training can help make these types of sparring situations more productive for all involved by allowing the more experienced fighter to train with a less experienced fighter while simultaneously benefitting both. TID can easily assign the more experienced fighter techniques he is less familiar or less effective with each round. For example, have a right-handed fighter use only his or her left side. Or have a kicker use only hand techniques while the less experienced fighter gets to use his or her very best techniques. Many times this helps to level the playing field and provides a mutually beneficial exchange as the more experienced fighter hones his lesser developed skills and the less experienced fighter gets to fine-tune his strengths. The less experienced fighter gains confidence, knowing that the more experienced fighter is limited to his less effective tools (and will not annihilate him). The less experienced fighter can begin to get the feel of scoring with his best techniques while at the same time improving them. Ultimately, this allows for a more productive training session as each fighter now can offer tangible value against the other.

Takes the Competeiveness Out of Training

TID is designed to take the competitiveness out of sparring. Typically, sparring tends to lead to some level of competition even when it's in *"practice mode."* While competition is often viewed as a good motivator, it can sometimes interfere with the learning process at the fundamental levels. The main goal of TID is to isolate single attacking techniques through repetition. TID aims to familiarize a fighter with a technique so that identification and reaction to that technique becomes more of a reflex. For TID to be most effective, it should be treated as a drill/learning tool instead of a contest to best your opponent.

Map first, isolate second! These two strategies complement each other well!

Using technique mapping and TID training together is highly recommended and an excellent way to improve your overall sparring ability. Technique mapping will first tell you what techniques should be used. TID will help develop your physical ability to actually apply the techniques in a sparring match.

Chapter 18:
Sparring at Tournament

Sparring at tournament is very different from sparring in the dojo. Although you spend many hours sparring in preparation for competition, it is very difficult to completely simulate the entire tournament experience in the dojo alone. This chapter will help you better prepare for tournaments by outlining key points to consider when sparring in open competition (including commonalities within the sport, such as calls and hand signals used by the officials) and provide tips and strategies that will better prepare you for tournament competition.

Ring Size

The size of the ring varies from tournament to tournament. Generally, the ring size is 20 ft. x 20 ft. but can be smaller (especially for children's divisions). The ring borders are usually designated with 1 in.+ wide tape (or sometimes painted). Starting lines are usually about 6 ft. apart in the middle of the ring. Each ring is posted with a ring number, which should be visible to the competitors, officials, spectators and medical personnel.

Official Sparring Calls and Hand Signals

Like most organized sports, point sparring utilizes a series of pre-determined combinations of hand signals and verbal calls to communicate various elements of the match to the competitors and the audience. They can be broken down into three main categories: (1.) bout management, (2.) scoring and (3.) penalties. Much like the general Sport Karate rule set, the calls and hand signals used by officials can vary from tournament to tournament. The methods for how they are delivered can also differ. In some competitions, the judges use whistles and flags; in others they simply use their hands. The following are a sampling (based on the World Martial Arts Championships [WMAC] rule set) of the more common calls and hand signals used at most Sport Karate point sparring competitions. Some officials may use both verbal calls and hand signals together; others tend to favor verbal commands over hand signals, using mainly their voice to officiate the match (in conjunction with just the most basic hand signals). The calls and signals presented in this section do not represent all possible calls and signals that may exist nor do they represent the many variations that may be encountered. Some tournaments may use dozens of hand signals and calls whereas others may just have a handful. It is incumbent on the competitor to fully understand not only the sparring rules for the tournament he or she is competing in but also the calls and hand signals that will be used.

Bout Management Signals

The Bow to Officials (at the beginning and end of a match)

"Attention"

"Competitors"
(palms facing the competitors)

"Face the Referee"

"Bow"

Competitors Bow to Each Other (at the beginning and end of a match)

"Attention"

"Competitors"

"Bow to each other"

Inviting Competitors to Enter the Ring

Palms facing competitors, walk forward

Bring hands together palms facing each other

Stop at referee position with hands approximately 1 – 2 fist lengths apart

Checking Officials and Starting the Match

Judges ready?

Table ready? (front view) If there is a judging table present…

Table ready? (view from the table)

Step forward with one foot and your front hand raised to about head level. Say "Begin" in a loud voice, while simultaneously sliding the same foot back to its original position and move the hand in a downward slicing motion.

Stop and Continue

"Stop!"
(when a point, penalty,
or end of bout occurs)

"Competitors, back
to starting position
and get ready."

"Competitors Start!"
(after points or penalties have been awarded)

Stopping the Clock/Time Out

This is generally done by the referee but may also be done by a corner judge if the referee is occupied. This hand signal is sometimes accompanied with the verbal phrase "Time-out."

Scoring Calls and Signals

When the referee believes there has been a significant exchange of techniques, or when signaled to do so by a corner judge(s), he or she will call out the word *"Stop!"* in a loud voice. The referee then returns the competitors to their starting marks and addresses the judges by saying *"Judges call!"* All judges and the center referee cast their votes simultaneously to determine whether a point was scored. The decision that has the majority vote wins.

Judges Call!

A point will be indicated with the hand held out, open, palm down at a 45-degree angle from the body on the scoring competitor's side of the ring.

Variations (not pictured):

- Officials will sometimes indicate the number of points scored using their fingers.
- The positioning of the official arm may vary (not always on a 45-degree angle). The main consistency is the arm is always pointed toward the fighter who scored.

No Score

Indicated by crossing the forearms in front of the body, hands open, palms down, waving them back and forth in a scissor-like manner.

Judges Please Approach

There may be times during a match that require an official's conference. This is indicated by the referee extending his hands out, palms down toward the judges. Rotate the hands and bring them in toward the referee's face. This gesture essentially says, "You, please come here," with each hand.

Variations to the No Score Signal

Some tournaments will use more descriptive hand signals to better communicate the exact reason for the point not being awarded. Here are some of the most common examples.

Did Not See

Placing the hands over the eyes, palms facing inward, signifies that the point was not seen clearly by the official and therefore not awarded.

Clash

Knuckles of both fists together at chest level, forearms parallel to the ground. This signifies that both competitors scored simultaneously and therefore no point is awarded.

Blocked

Is indicated by bending one arm, hand up and open and lightly tapping the elbow/lower section of the forearm with the fingers of the other hand. This signifies that a strike was blocked or hit a non-target area and therefore no point is awarded.

Declaring the Result of the Match

At the conclusion of a bout, both fighters return to their starting marks and wait for the result of the match to be declared by the referee.

Winner

The referee will sharply sweep his or her hand up at a 45-degree angle pointing toward the appropriate side. The referee will also simultaneously verbally indicate the result of the bout.

Draw

In case of a draw, the hand signal used will be open hands crossed over at waist height, palms outward. The referee will also simultaneously verbally indicate the result of the bout. In most tournaments, a draw will result in a 2-minute "sudden death" extension round. If no point is scored in the first sudden death extension round, a second extension round will be fought (until a point is scored).

Penalty Calls and Signals

When the referee believes a foul has been committed or when signaled to do so by a corner judge(s), he or she calls out the word *"Stop!"* in a loud voice. The referee then returns the competitors to their starting marks and addresses the judges by saying *"Judges call!"* All judges and the center referee then cast their votes simultaneously as to whether or not a foul was committed. If the foul is a second or third offense (within the same match), the same format would be used determine if the competitor is to be disqualified. The decision that has the majority vote wins.

Penalty

To signify a penalty, the official will point and circle his or her index finger straight up in the air. The official then points his or her other hand at the fighter who committed the foul.

1st Point Penalty

The referee will point to the competitor's waist with his index finger and also verbally announce "First penalty." This is followed up by awarding a point to the opponent or taking away a point from the fighter who committed the penalty.

2nd Point Penalty

The referee will point to the competitor's upper area (neck/face) and verbally announce "Second penalty." Since this is an escalated penalty, the area the referee points to visually changes to reflect the escalation. This is followed by awarding a point to the opponent or taking away a point from the fighter who committed the penalty.

Disqualification

Disqualifications typically occur after two official warnings (with point deductions), but can also immediately result with a flagrant or excessive rule violation. The referee will point to the competitor's neck/face area again saying "Disqualified." The referee will then back out, pointing approximately 30 to 45 degrees behind himself on the disqualified competitor's side. This gesture essentially points the fighter off the mat.

Variations to the Penalty Signal

Some tournaments will use additional, more descriptive hand signals to better communicate the precise reason for a penalty, warning or disqualification. Here are some of the most common examples.

Attack with Head, Knees or Elbows

Attack with or to the head is signified by the gesture of the fist to the cheek

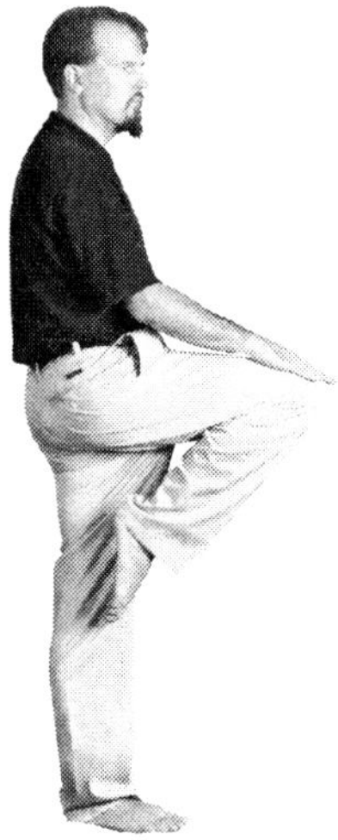

Attack with the knee is represented by lifting and patting the knee.

Attack with the elbow is represented by patting the elbow to simulate an elbow strike.

Pushing

This is indicated by the referee bringing the hands to shoulder level and pushing straight out.

Grabbing

The official will indicate grabbing by holding his or her forearm and pulling it with the other hand. This signal applies to any form of grabbing.

Avoiding Combat

Purposley avoiding fighting can result in penalty (or even disqualification). This is indicated by the official pointing his or her index finger down, and just off to the side, and rotating his or her entire arm, suggesting that the fighter is running around in circles.

Clock Management

Clock management is a vital element in Sport Karate sparring but too many competitors do not factor it into their overall sparring strategy. It can sometimes be the difference between winning and losing (especially in very evenly matched engagements). The following tips should be considered regarding clock management:

Be Efficient

In most tournaments, you only have 2 minutes to either win by scoring the maximum points (usually 3 to 5 points) or scoring more points than your opponent within that 2-minute timeframe. The best way to maximize your effort is by scoring with head kicks. Head kicks in many tournaments are worth 2 points whereas body shots and hand techniques are only worth 1 point per hit. Two quick successful head kicks can put a match almost out of reach immediately and put your opponent into a precarious position very early in the match. By the same token, if you are behind on points and time is winding down, head kicks can quickly put you back into the lead.

Time Awareness

Be aware of how much time is left in the match. Your strategy will be dictated by a combination of the score and the time remaining. If you are up on points late in the match, your strategy becomes more about sticking, moving and keeping your distance (to allow the clock to run out) and, in the worst case, using a body kick or hand technique to keep on opponent out of range. On the other hand, if you are down on points and time is running out, your strategy is about scoring the maximum number of points as quickly as possible. This will require some urgency on your part with more risky/difficult techniques, like head kicks. Some very gifted competitors possess the ability to keep track of time in their head. Most competitors need to rely on a teammate or coach to help them (by calling it out, etc.).

Score Awareness

It may seem silly, but you need to keep track of the score in your mind. The score in conjunction with the time remaining will dictate your immediate strategy. Some competitors can get so preoccupied with the match that they lose track of the score. The ability to multitask is an unwritten requirement of being a successful point fighter. Never lose track of the score! If you do, ask for the score when the referee breaks the action or have your coach yell it from the sidelines every once in a while during the course of the match.

Ring Management

Ring Management is another important consideration in your overall tournament sparring strategy. In most tournaments, there are 4 judges, one at each corner of the ring. They are outside the ring fixed to their position. The referee stands inside the ring and is permitted to move around with the fighters the entire duration of the match. Good competitors know how to use the ring to their advantage. They direct their attacks to force their opponent out of bounds. They are also aware of and careful not to step out of bounds themselves or to run into the referee. Most importantly, they know how to execute techniques so the majority of the officials can clearly see their point. This is critical because if you are positioned incorrectly, you could legitimately score but not be awarded the point because the majority of the officials did not get a clear view of the technique hitting your opponent. It's always good to position yourself so your opponent's point zone is visible to at least 2 judges and the referee. This concept also works in reverse. If your back faces 2 or 3 judges, a body shot from your opponent may not be called. To minimize the risk of having your attack go unnoticed, try using techniques that are most visible to all officials regardless of your opponent's position. Typically, head shots are more noticeable than body shots. The actual delivery of a technique can also make the difference between receiving a point and not. Variations to the ridge hand, for example, are a perfect example. The vertical ridge hand is a deliberate point fighting modification to a traditional technique for purposes of being more easily recognized by the majority of officials in competition.

Most sparring divisions consist of 4 corner judges and 1 referee. The corner judges are fairly fixed to their positions and do not move much, whereas the referee can move around the ring along with the fighters.

Front view

Reverse view

A good ring management strategy is to try to position yourself so your attack is visible to the majority of the officials. Above, the fighter on the left legitimately scores with a round kick to the body; however her position is such that only 2 of the 5 officials could clearly see it. The result is that a point would not be awarded.

A

B

Head shots are generally more visible to a greater number of officials then body shots (A, B). Head shots can often help negate poor positioning (i.e., attacking from a bad angle often results in body attacks not being adequately seen by the majority of the officials, resulting in points not being awarded).

The photo above illustrates how scoring with a body kick is not always as obvious to the majority of the officials.

Following up kicking techniques with hand strikes is a good rule of thumb in the Sport Karate game. (1.) In this sequence, the attacker (right) initiates a lead leg round kick to the body. (2.) The defender (left) retreats backward as she switches her stance in an effort to avoid the attack. However, the attacker continues to press forward, targeting her opponent's head with a hammer fist, which successfully scores.

Techniques can be modified so they are more effective for competition. In the following example, the traditional ridge hand strike to the head is made more visible to all the officials by changing the angle of delivery (from a horizontal trajectory to a vertical one).

Horizontal Ridge Hand Strike *(less visible)*

Vertical Ridge Hand Strike *(more visible)*

Energy Management

Successful fighters know how to pace themselves at tournament. If you plan to win, you will have to fight multiple matches against different opponents, so learning how to pace the fight is critical. Don't tire yourself quickly, because it will negatively affect your speed, power and ability to think! Beginners tend to rush in and expend everything they have in the opening 30 to 40 seconds of their first fight. If they fail to end the fight in that time, they often find themselves fatigued, with their ability to fight greatly diminished. Such cases generally result in a fighter losing the match or, at the very least, the next match. A high percentage of your overall offensive techniques should be comprised of low risk/high scoring percentage type of attacks such as the back fist and round kick. This will allow you to score in the most economic manner while not exposing yourself to unnecessary risk and premature fatigue. While more complex techniques tend to please the crowd, they are not advised because they have a lower scoring percentage, require greater levels of energy and, if they fail to connect, leave you unreasonably susceptible to counter-attack. It is also important to monitor the number of techniques you are executing per match. Even low risk techniques require energy to execute. Concentrate on executing fewer but more accurate and appropriate techniques to legal target areas. Winning a match does not require you to use hundreds of kicks and punches; fewer, more precise attacks can often lead to victory while also leaving you with enough energy for the later matches.

Emotional Control

It is important that you maintain emotional control when fighting. Fear, anger, self-doubt and arrogance can derail the efforts of even the most physically talented fighter. These negative emotions cloud your mind, which results in diminished physical performance. Lack of emotional control can impact your performance much the same as being exhausted, physically injured or just lacking in a specific skill set. It can instantly erase any advantages you may have over your opponent. It is always important to remember that point fighting is just a game. If it causes you too much emotional distress, you should work toward increasing control over your emotions and eradicating any negative emotions. If this is not possible, you should refrain from competition until you have the ability to do so. Some fighters will intentionally try to *"get into the heads"* of their opponents and purposely invoke negative emotions (such as anger, fear and frustration). They use this as part of their fighting strategy, knowing how effective it is in diminishing their opponent's physical capabilities and giving them an advantage. **Do not allow yourself to fall victim to this!**

Follow Up

A common mistake, and one that is easy to avoid, is to stop attacking after you feel you have scored a point. Until the referee interrupts the action, the fight is still happening and you can be hit and scored upon. Therefore, you must continue until the ref jumps in. Always exercise caution and control, however, so you don't continue to strike after a break has been called. Otherwise, you may be penalized.

Don't React to Being Hit

If your opponent successfully hits you, do not react to the hit. You should behave as if the strike missed or hit a non-scoring area and continue sparring until the referee signals to break. Sometimes, the officials may not actually see a technique land, but based on your reaction (i.e., stopping, returning to the line or even verbally confirming the point out loud – "nice point") to a hit (even if it didn't land) can result in the officials erroneously awarding your opponent a point. This is particularly true with more oblique attacks to the body or attacks that are delivered on bad angles (from the judge's viewpoint). The reverse is also true; you may legitimately get hit, but if you do not react to it and keep fighting the officials may not call it.

Be Loud

Another way to maximize your ability to score is to be loud. People naturally react to loud noises. When you are executing any scoring technique, particularly to the more obscure body targets, issue a strong *kiap*. In the game of inches, the noise you make could mean the difference between winning and losing.

Be Observant

There is a lot of down time between events at most tournaments. A smart fighter will use this time to study his or her potential opponents. You should watch them warm up and work out before the matches. If they are competing in forms divisions (which usually occur first), study their technique. Do they move fast, do they have the ability to effectively kick head level, are they nervous? In many tournaments you know very little about the opponent(s) you are fighting prior to the match. The more recon you do before you step into the ring, the better prepared you will be. Most importantly, once the fighting divisions begin, watch intently every fight in your division (and even those outside your division if your goal is a grand championship). Absorb as much information about potential opponents as you can. Remember, even if you do not fight a particular opponent that day, chances are you might see him or her again in future tournaments. Learn as much about their strengths and vulnerabilities. Watch for specifics such as: kicking proficiency, favored techniques, overall physical endurance, and mental toughness (can you get into their head? are they fighting emotionally?) and, most importantly, take note of what techniques are working for them. If you intend to fight on a tournament circuit, you may want to consider video recording the fight (if the tournament permits) to better catalog your observations.

Chapter 19: How to Introduce Sparring to New Students

When introducing sparring to new students it is absolutely essential that it be done correctly, as the initial sparring introduction can literally make the difference between a student becoming a competitor or quitting the martial arts altogether. Fear is usually a new student's main concern. This is mainly because the student simply does not know what to do. Many new to sparring also erroneously believe they will be injured or will injure others. While this is always a possibility, when students adhere to the rules, wear the proper safety gear and spar under expert supervision, point sparring is actually safer than most sports. When working with students new to sparring, it is important to empower them with knowledge. When they know what to do and what to expect, they can begin to enjoy and excel in point sparring. This is best done in stages using a phased learning approach.

Stage 1

Explain and demonstrate the technique or concept so that it is completely understood by the student at his or her intellectual level.

Stage 2

Begin to have the student practice the technique on his or her own in the air. The emphasis should be on proper mechanics, body positioning, stance and footwork. Start slowly and gradually increase the speed and intensity as the student becomes more familiar with the technique.

Stage 3

Once the student is comfortable with executing the technique in the air, focus pads, air shields and heavy bags can help with fine-tuning.

Stage 4

Next, the technique should be applied in controlled sparring drills (such as TID or Line Sparring).

Stage 5

Controlled free sparring: Spar slowly and stop after each exchange to analyze the effectiveness (or ineffectiveness) of the technique. Provide advice on how to improve the technique for greater success. Allow for multiple concepts to be used simultaneously (i.e., back fist and kicks, etc.).

Stage 6

Spar at normal pace without stopping to analyze each exchange. Any analysis should be done at the end when the round or sparring has been completed.

TIPS!

- Never progress to a new stage prematurely. You must be comfortable with the technique and demonstrate proficiency at the earlier level before moving to the next level.
- It is important to teach that the intent of point sparring is not to hurt or injure the opponent, but to score points. Non-continuous point sparring is like a game of tag, and it is a sport with specific rules.
- Show empathy to students who display a fear of sparring. Sparring can be frightening or unnatural at first, especially for younger students. Knowledge is the key to conquering fear. Once the student has learned what to do he or she is in control and fear is diminished!
- The use of *"Technique Mapping"* and *"Technique Isolation Drills"* are great tools for teaching point sparring to new students.
- Practice makes perfect! Make sure the student understands that mastery is achieved through understanding and repetition. It is equally important to realize that mastery will not be instantaneous and will require time and effort.
- If a student is doing the technique wrong, immediately stop and correct. Otherwise, the student may internalize the technique incorrectly, which ultimately leads to more work (unlearning the wrong method and relearning the proper method).
- Motivation is important; always find something positive to praise (no matter how insignificant).
- Encourage a student whenever possible. The use of humor sometimes defuses tense or frustrating situations and makes the learning process smoother and more enjoyable.
- Be patient. Not every student progresses at the same pace. A good instructor/coach realizes this and works accordingly with the competitor.
- Match sparring partners accordingly. You should know your student's capabilities. Initially, you should avoid placing aggressive fighters with timid ones. Allow timid fighters to gain confidence before facing the more aggressive fighter.

Chapter 20: Conclusion

Point sparring is a dynamic and exciting sport practiced by martial artists of all ages around the world. Unlike other fighting sports, point sparring's main objective is to quickly outscore the opponent rather than to submit or knock him or her out. Speed and agility reign supreme, as it is all about who can hit the target first.

I hope you have found something useful in this book. I have tried to provide a wide and complete range of content about this topic to reach and benefit the broadest audience possible. One final thought on point sparring: It is important to have fun with it. Whether you are a national competitor or just sparring in your dojo, point fighting should provide enjoyment. Becoming a better point fighter requires dedication and hard work. If you do not derive enjoyment from this activity, you will invariably be less dedicated and not put in the work required for improvement. It is a game, so have fun.

Good luck with your training!

Biography

Ed Yuncza is a Trenton, New Jersey-based professional martial artist with more than 25 years of training. He is the owner and chief instructor of E.Y. Martial Arts & Self-Defense Concepts, L.L.C. located in Mercerville, New Jersey.

Ed is also an inducted member of both the U.S.A. Martial Arts Hall of Fame and Action Martial Arts Magazine's Hall of Honors. He is a frequent contributor to Black Belt Magazine and has been writing for the magazine since 1995. He has also written for other martial arts publications such as Inside Kung Fu magazine.

Ed holds a 5th degree black belt in the Superfoot System under Grandmaster Bill Wallace, a 5th degree black belt in American Taekwondo under Master John Graden and a 4th degree black belt in WTF Taekwondo (Kukkiwon certified) as well as teaching certificates under Grandmaster Richard Chun and Master Sang H. Kim. He also holds a 4th degree black belt in the Okinawan/American based system of Gu Ju Dao Te Karate Do under Master Jeffrey A. Mack and is an Apprentice Instructor in Jeet Kune Do Concepts under Sifu Paul Vunak. In addition, he is an NRA certified firearms instructor and a licensed C.O.B.R.A. self-defense instructor.

Ed has been employed in the Information Technology field since the mid 1990s and currently works as an IT Manager at Princeton University. When he is not working, he enjoys spending time with his family.

For more information please visit
www.eymartialarts.com

Acknowledgements

Chapter 4: The Tools

- Yuncza, Ed. "10 Commandments of Kicking". *Black Belt* Dec. 2006:108-115.

Chapter 11: Defense

- Yuncza, Ed. "Counter-Kicks". *Black Belt* Apr. 2008:108-113.

Chapter 14: Sparring Drills

- Yuncza, Ed. "Special Sparring Drills". *Black Belt* Mar. 1996:30, 31, 33, 120.

Chapter 18: Sparring at Tournaments

- Yuncza, Ed. "Going for the Gold". *Black Belt* Oct. 2001:94-99.

INDEX

T

U

V

W

Z

NOTES

Notes

Notes